BAUDELAIRE

La Fanfarlo *and*
Le Spleen de Paris

Barbara Wright

Professor of French Literature
Trinity College, Dublin

and

David H.T. Scott

Lecturer in French
Trinity College, Dublin

Grant & Cutler Ltd
1984

© Grant & Cutler Ltd
1984
ISBN 0 7293 0176 1

I.S.B.N. 84-499-6919-0

DEPÓSITO LEGAL: V. 219 - 1984

Printed in Spain by
Artes Gráficas Soler, S.A., Valencia
for
GRANT & CUTLER LTD
11 BUCKINGHAM STREET, LONDON W.C.2

For Alison Fairlie

Contents

Preface

The aim of this volume is to encourage interest in two less well known works by the author of *Les Fleurs du Mal*: the early novella, *La Fanfarlo*, and the prose poems of *Le Spleen de Paris*. Although these two studies differ in their approach — reflecting both the different nature of the two works and the individual temperaments of the two writers on them — it is hoped that both will, nevertheless, lead to a deeper understanding of Baudelaire the writer at two crucial stages in his career: the period before 1847 and that of the early eighteen-sixties.

Separate footnotes and bibliography accompany each of the two studies but both have adopted, as far as possible, a similar system of reference. While several paperback editions of *Le Spleen de Paris* exist (e.g. Livre de Poche, Garnier-Flammarion; see bibliography, p.90), there is no available paperback version of *La Fanfarlo*. All references to Baudelaire's writings other than the correspondence are therefore to his *Œuvres complètes* (ed. Claude Pichois, Bibliothèque de la Pléiade, 2 vols, 1975-76). Except in the case of *Le Spleen de Paris* and the occasional allusion to *Les Fleurs du Mal*, where the titles of individual poems will be given, all such references will give the volume number, followed by the page number(s), e.g. (I, 561). References to the works listed in the two bibliographies give the number (in italics) of the edition, book or article, followed by the page number(s), e.g. (*32*, p.24).

B.W., D.H.T.S.

La Fanfarlo

Introduction

Ambivalence surrounds virtually everything concerned with *La Fanfarlo*. First published in January 1847 in the periodical *Bulletin de la Société des gens de lettres*, the precise date of its composition is the source of disagreement among scholars. It was probably written some time between 1843 and the end of 1846 (see I, 1414).

The autobiographical links, likewise, are tantalisingly elusive. If Asselineau and Gautier were among the first of many authoritative commentators to reach unanimity on the striking resemblance, physical and otherwise, between Samuel Cramer and Baudelaire himself, the parallelism with Emile Deroy (1820-46) is none the less significant (see *22*). Deroy's early portrait of Baudelaire is probably the best visual representation available of the quasi-fictitious Samuel Cramer. Furthermore, since Baudelaire did not become acquainted with Delacroix until March 1846, Emile Deroy is now thought to have been Baudelaire's aesthetic mentor in the period leading up to *Le Salon de 1845*; his possible influence on the artistic views expressed by Samuel Cramer is therefore far from negligible.

In 1842, Baudelaire first met Jeanne Duval, then an actress at the Théâtre de la Porte Saint-Antoine. She may thus be one of the possible sources of inspiration for the dancer in *La Fanfarlo*. So too may Marie Daubrun, an actress at the Théâtre Montmartre from autumn 1845, whose influence in this connection has been explored by Claude Pichois (see *11*, *3*, and I, 1414). Recent researches (see *18*) have shown, however, that Baudelaire may have written *La Fanfarlo*, along with *Choix de maximes consolantes sur l'amour* (1846), at least partially as a tongue-in-cheek homage to Félicité Baudelaire (see I, 1414 and *3*, pp. 23-25). Félicité Baudelaire was the wife of Baudelaire's half-brother, Alphonse, from whom he sought vengeance for having been 'betrayed' on several counts: having at first got on

well with his half-brother, Baudelaire subsequently held the
latter responsible for collusion with his hated stepfather,
General Aupick, in having him sent abroad on a long journey
(1841-42); for divulging confidences about his incipient syphilis;
and for contributing towards his disinheritance. In the two years
after attaining his majority, Baudelaire had spent about half the
money bequeathed to him by his father. His family, seeking to
have the balance held in trust for him, proceeded to have a
'conseil judiciaire' appointed in September 1844, with Maître
Ancelle as the lawyer in charge. Baudelaire was humiliated by
this experience, which, in the view of Michel Butor, morally, at
least, emasculated him (*14*, p. 79). In 1845, having left
everything to Jeanne Duval, Baudelaire attempted suicide.

Neither the author's name, nor even the title of the novella, is
free of deliberate ambiguity. When published in 1847, *La
Fanfarlo* was signed by Charles Defayis, 'Defayis' being the
maiden name of Baudelaire's mother. And the title? Despite
many suggestions, it still retains all the mystery of a conundrum.
There are possible associations with a polka-dancer of the time,
called Fanfarnou (*2*, pp.165-66); or, more simply still, the name
may derive from the substantive 'fanfare' (see I, 1422, n.1 to
p.566); but what is perhaps most fascinating of all is the sound
of the name, combining the feminine ending 'a' with the
masculine ending 'o'. Typically, too, the title of the novella is
not clarified until the tale is well advanced, a technique which
Baudelaire will later use in the prose poem, 'Un Cheval de race'.

As Baudelaire himself said in relation to E.T.A. Hoffmann,
Samuel Cramer, the protagonist in *La Fanfarlo*, is 'atteint d'un
dualisme chronique' (II, 542). This dual nature[1] is highlighted,
from the outset, by the fact that Samuel Cramer once wrote
under a feminine pseudonym, Manuela de Monteverde, as
Mérimée had done in *Le Théâtre de Clara Gazul* (see I, 1417, n.1
to p.553). Even though these names may be seen to have

---

[1] Baudelaire used the phrase 'atteint d'un dualisme chronique' to describe Giglio
Fava, the protagonist in E.T.A. Hoffmann's *Prinzessin Brambilla*, a novella
which presents many affinities with *La Fanfarlo*. The theme of the double is
central to both works; however, Rosemary Lloyd wisely cautions against
identifying Samuel Cramer as a *Doppelgänger*: 'il représente la lutte morale de
l'individu contre des penchants qui tendent à l'avilir' (*17*, p.93).

emanated from a single source,[2] they nevertheless point to a fundamental duality within the protagonist.

However, this duality, this ambivalence, is, for the most part, a reflection of Baudelaire's conscious and deliberate intention: it is at the core of his early dramatic work, *Idéolus* (started in 1843, in association with Ernest Prarond), the plot of which has many parallels with *La Fanfarlo*. In a manner less impish than Gide's subsequent refusal to be pinned down to any one specific attitude if that were necessarily to preclude its opposite, Baudelaire's work involves a series of swings of the pendulum, encompassing, at one and the same time, attitudes and expressions which might often be seen as mutually exclusive. This is mirrored in his use of form, where he builds up patterns and expectations and then introduces shock tactics, concluding with some quite unexpected turn, after what might have been thought to prefigure a harmonious resolution of suspense.

Duality pervades *La Fanfarlo*, in which, thematically and structurally, the binary movement is predominant. For the purposes of this brief study, two sets of polar opposites will be distinguished, as areas of possible emphasis in further work on the subject, rather than as neat categories:

1. Duality within the double narrative sequence, the first sequence being that in which the protagonist, Samuel Cramer, presented as a latter-day knight-errant, ends by setting out on a mission for his *belle dame sans merci*, Mme de Cosmelly (I, 555-69); the second sequence being that in which Samuel Cramer, in seeking to woo the dancer, La Fanfarlo, away from Mme de Cosmelly's husband, succeeds in falling in love with her himself, thus getting caught in a trap of his own making, since it was with the ulterior motive of obtaining a 'reward' from Mme de Cosmelly that Samuel Cramer had embarked on the venture in the first place (I, 570-79).

2. Duality inherent in the narrator's attitude towards his discourse.

---

[2] It was Jean Pommier (*19*, pp. 90-92) who turned up the volume '*Il vivere*, par Samuel Bach, libraire' (1836), which, in addition to this reference to 'Samuel', also pays tribute, among others, to the German pianist, J.B. Cramer. A second volume, *Les Romans et le mariage* (1837), provides the author's name retrospectively (Théophile de Ferrière) and also has a character named 'de Montevède', an almost exact antecedent of 'de Monteverde'.

1. La Fanfarlo: *duality within the double narrative sequence*

Between the first and second narrative sequences, there is a relationship of call and echo which heightens the effect of their juxtaposition, allowing for ironic interplay between the two, coupled with constant shifts in the point of view of the narrator.

The first narrative sequence involves an overt parody of first-generation Romanticism, while adopting many of the stances of Balzac as omniscient narrator and of Stendhal as ironic deflator.

Four encounters, in all, are involved in the development of Samuel Cramer's relationship with Mme de Cosmelly. From his studious attic, his typically elevated 'prison romantique' ('du haut de sa solitude' (I, 555)), Samuel had seen and admired Mme de Cosmelly, whom he remembered from his provincial days in Lyon. Leaving his bedside reading, which included some Swedenborg (often hailed as the 'link' between Balzac's 'langage des fleurs' and Baudelaire's later development of the aesthetics of 'correspondances'), Samuel attired himself elegantly, as Rastignac might have done before him, and set out to contrive an encounter with Mme de Cosmelly. This meeting takes place on neutral ground, in a public park. By contrast, in the second narrative sequence, Samuel will seek out La Fanfarlo in the intimacy of her back-stage dressing-room and, later, in her private apartment. With Mme de Cosmelly, he never progresses beyond the bench in the Luxembourg Gardens.

The first encounter with Mme de Cosmelly serves, therefore, to establish identity. Samuel, recalling how they had grown up together in Lyon, assembles 'tout ce jeune roman' (I, 556) which, in the hands of a more conventional author, might have been the pretext for the development of a sub-plot of some sort. Mme de Cosmelly, in consultation with her maid-servant, recognizes Samuel. This establishment of identities is again in contrast with the necessarily more oblique way in which Samuel will make himself known to the dancer, La Fanfarlo, by writing reviews of her performances in terms so scathing that her professional reputation requires her to find out more about one who is ostensibly so hostile towards her.

The second encounter is contrived by Mme de Cosmelly, who adopts the fairly standard ploy of leaving her book and her handkerchief on the bench, thus affording Samuel the pretext of returning these to her. Later, he will seek to develop his relationship with Mme de Cosmelly by offering her his collection of sonnets and by responding to her reaction to his work which we, as readers, know only indirectly. Again, in the intermediary section between the two principal narrative sequences (I, 569-70), we learn how Samuel will offer sonnets to both Mme de Cosmelly and La Fanfarlo, confusing, ironically, the addressees.

The development takes place through oblique means in both narrative sequences. In the course of the second encounter with Mme de Cosmelly, Samuel launches into an attack on Walter Scott, the author of the novel left behind by Mme de Cosmelly. In his *Conseils aux jeunes littérateurs* (1846), Baudelaire distinguishes, in criticism, between two methods of slating: 'éreintage...par la ligne courbe, et par la ligne droite, qui est le plus court chemin' (II, 16). Both the narrative sequences in *La Fanfarlo* contain such 'éreintage': the target is Scott, in the first instance (a sally not without its boomerang effect on his disciple, Balzac); in the second, it is La Fanfarlo herself. In terms of plot, the effect of both is similar, in that a pretext has been found for entering into a more personal phase in the separate relationships. There is, however, this difference that the 'writing', in the second narrative sequence, is unashamedly journalistic, whereas in the first it is pretentiously literary, with Samuel undertaking to offer Mme de Cosmelly his collection of sonnets, *Les Orfraies*, on the following day, the occasion of their third encounter.

The fourth and final encounter with Mme de Cosmelly centres, primarily, on her reaction to *Les Orfraies*. In Samuel's work, she criticizes many of the devices which were not merely characteristic of the period, but which will re-appear in the second narrative sequence, in the context of La Fanfarlo. By contrast with Mme de Cosmelly, who, in the first narrative sequence, had been described in only the vaguest of terms ('ses traits...avaient la grâce profonde et décente de l'honnête femme' (I, 556)), La Fanfarlo is described with all the hyperbole so castigated earlier on. Yet, conversely, the force of this hyperbole is undercut, in terms of its ironic impact, by virtue of Mme de Cosmelly's previous condemnation. In language which is often 'mystique', as well as sensuous and exotic, La Fanfarlo, projected as the Dancer, is evoked in terms reminiscent of both 'des créatures bizarres' and 'des sultanes de bas lieu' (I, 559). The scene in which, anticipating the ballet-dancers of Degas by over twenty years, La Fanfarlo, is leaning over to lace up her boots, is suggestive of a geometrical pattern, pin-pointed in terms both mathematical and anatomical: 'Tranchée perpendiculairement à l'endroit le plus large, cette jambe eût donné une espèce de triangle dont le sommet eût été sur le tibia, et dont la ligne arrondie du mollet eût fourni la base convexe'. Again, in her bent posture, 'sa tête, inclinée vers son pied...laissait deviner l'ornière des omoplates' (I, 572). All of this constitutes an ironic echo of Mme de Cosmelly's earlier rejection of Samuel's 'descriptions d'anatomie' (I, 559). Furthermore, Mme de Cosmelly deplores the poet's adulation of the feet and hands of his mistress when, according to strict bourgeois ethics, a woman should be knitting socks and mittens for her children's feet and hands; in the second narrative sequence, the narrator, with ironical detachment, gives an account of Samuel's behaviour when first received in the home of La Fanfarlo: 'Notre homme exprimait son admiration par des baisers muets qu'il lui appliquait avec ferveur sur les pieds et les mains' (I, 574).

The observations by Mme de Cosmelly provoke a torrent of Romantic outpouring on the part of Samuel, punctuated at four points (I, 561-62): the first, where Mme de Cosmelly seeks to deflect his attention to the springtime flowers in the park; the second, where she is unable to get in a word edgeways; the third, where Samuel is cut short by the realization of the hurt being caused to her by his rhetorical monologue; and the fourth, where she weeps and her tears lead to a double mis-understanding, with role-playing involved on both sides (her 'candide désolation' ironically underscoring the 'mission' with which she will shortly proceed to charge her gallant knight-errant, and his hypocritical pride at having been able to move her to tears, as he thought, seeing in the emotion of the percipient 'son œuvre et sa propriété littéraire'). The four set pieces, thus punctuated, are essentially displays of 'jargon romantique' (I, 569) and are followed by a fifth, in the hypocritically didactic vein characterized by the term 'patois séminariste'. Together, they form a marked contrast with the 'Oui, Madame' (I, 572), uttered by Samuel to La Fanfarlo in the second narrative sequence; his earlier outpourings to Mme de Cosmelly are here recalled in terms of one who had 'bavardé comme une pie romantique'.

It is, perhaps, not without significance that Baudelaire who, in the last analysis, is remembered primarily for his outstanding achievement in verse poetry, chose to have Samuel 'mettre en prose et...déclamer quelques mauvaises stances composées dans sa première manière' (I, 560). His attempts seem deliberately pedestrian and contrast with the more poetic prose contained in parts of the second narrative sequence. In general terms, it is agreed that verse pre-dates prose in the creative imagination of Baudelaire (see *21*, pp.174-76; *3*, p.105); but equally it is clear that, from the outset of his literary career, he was concerned to make a distinction between these two forms. Overt reference to an alexandrine, in *La Fanfarlo*, would seem to be rejected, as though for fear of making the writing seem that much more suspect as prose. In the second narrative sequence, there is an instance where the poetry reworked has been variously identified as that of Ernest Prarond or of Baudelaire himself, and where the original alexandrine would appear to have been wilfully distorted, metrically, as well as in terms of semantic context:

> Le ruisseau, lit funèbre où s'en vont les dégoûts (Original)
> Le ruisseau, lit funèbre où s'en vont les billets doux (I, 574).

The change, by Baudelaire, from 'dégoûts' to 'billets doux', is also indicative of his overall concern with ironic deflation in *La Fanfarlo*. Born into and yet reacting against the tradition of luxuriously poetic prose, as evolved by Rousseau and Chateaubriand, the future author of *Le Spleen de Paris* was already wanting to mark his originality in this art-form in which he was so clearly indebted to his precursors.

Again, in these passages declaimed by Samuel, 'à qui la phrase et la période étaient venues' (I, 560), some of the central themes of *Les Fleurs du Mal* are paralleled—ironically. There is, for example, an analogy with the poet of 'Bénédiction' in the following imprecation ('Bénédiction' was first published in 1857, but the date of its original composition may go back to the period 1844-46 (see *16*, p.344)): 'Malheur, trois fois malheur aux pères infirmes qui nous ont faits rachitiques et mal venus, prédestinés que nous sommes à n'enfanter que des morts-nés!' This is a reminder of the self-pitying introverts following in the wake of Chateaubriand's René and victims of the so-called 'mal du siècle'. Samuel differentiates his fellow-poets from ordinary mortals in the following terms: 'Ils vivent pour vivre, et nous, hélas! nous vivons pour savoir'. And yet the secret of Samuel's relative success in the second narrative sequence was precisely due to the fact that 'l'amour était chez lui moins une affaire des sens que du raisonnement' (I, 577).

The first narrative sequence concludes with Mme de Cosmelly's account, in terms reminiscent of Balzac's *Etudes de femme* and *Physiologie du mariage*, or, indeed, Baudelaire's own *Choix de maximes consolantes sur l'amour*, of how, since they had moved to Paris from the provinces, she had lost the love of her husband to a dancer, here named, for the first time (I, 566), as La Fanfarlo. This 'douleur de province' (I, 564) is simply told as 'une histoire banale, l'histoire de toutes les malheureuses,—un roman de province!' (I, 568). At the end of it all, thanks to the intervention of Samuel, whose eyes, it will be remembered, were 'brillants comme des gouttes de café' (I, 553), the reconciliation scene between husband and wife takes place after Mme de Cosmelly has prepared 'le meilleur thé du monde, dans une théière bien modeste et bien fêlée' (I, 578). Interestingly, however, when Mme de Cosmelly has recourse to artifice in order to try to regain her husband's affection (and before she has met Samuel again in Paris), she tarts herself up, 'la mort dans le cœur' (I, 568), in a way which prefigures the 'accoutrement fantasque' (I, 577) of La Fanfarlo: 'Moi, la chaste épouse qu'il était allé chercher au fond d'un pauvre château, j'ai paradé devant lui avec des robes de fille' (I, 567-68). La Fanfarlo's dancing costumes, made of 'étoffes...pailletées' (I, 571), are, to a small extent, anticipated in Mme de Cosmelly's admission to Samuel: 'J'ai pailleté mon désespoir avec des sourires étincelants. Hélas! il n'a rien vu' (I, 568). And, more obviously, the next remark by Mme de Cosmelly prefigures Samuel's almost hysterical request, in the seduction scene, that La Fanfarlo's Columbine costume be fetched, calling after her servant, Flore: 'Eh! n'oubliez pas le rouge!' (I, 577): 'J'ai mis du rouge, Monsieur, j'ai mis du rouge!' (I, 568). All to no avail, it would appear.

Between the two narrative sequences, there is thus continuity, cross-referencing and irony. Nowhere is this more evident than in the role-playing of all the protagonists, notably Samuel Cramer himself. Frequently characterized as a 'comédien', his play-acting in the first narrative sequence is mostly hypocritical. In the second, this is not so often the case, since he is described in less deprecatory terms. Endowed with some sense of originality (for La Fanfarlo, at any rate, he had 'l'attrait de la nouveauté' (I, 578)), he takes on what Nathaniel Wing has called 'the capacity to astonish' (*12*, p.182): '...avec ce diable d'homme, le grand problème est toujours de savoir où le comédien commence' (I, 572). This time, at least, Samuel was not 'ridicule' (I, 573).

It is in this more positive projection (with La Fanfarlo's art as a pendant to that of Samuel) that, despite continuing elements of irony, the couple here become 'le poète et la danseuse' (I, 574). Furthermore, far from the affected 'dandysme' (I, 566), which first offended Mme de Cosmelly in the gradual detachment of her husband, Samuel actually takes on the life-style of the *dandy* in the second narrative sequence, in terms which prefigure Baudelaire's later adumbrations on the subject in *Le Peintre de la vie moderne* (1863). He conducts his sensual life in the company of La Fanfarlo with the control of an actor or a poet. In short, the central difference in tone between the two narrative sequences is that, whereas, in the first, the predominant emphasis is on the parody of first-generation Romanticism, in the style of Gautier's *Les Jeunes-France*, in the second, there are elements of a continuing Romanticism which will pave the way for the later 'modernité' of Baudelaire, again as characterized in *Le Peintre de la vie moderne*: 'la beauté passagère, fugace, de la vie présente' (II, 724).

Typically, of course, Baudelaire will not be content to take comfort in the predictable swing of this binary movement from the first narrative sequence to the second, with all the sub-sets of call and echo subsumed in that structure. He will end the novella with a *pointe*, intended to disturb, if not to assault the reader, as he will do in some of the later prose poems. 'Intelligence malhonnête', he concludes, adding a throw-away line which is, in fact, a punch-line, '—comme dit cet honnête M. Nisard' (I, 580). In order to savour this *boutade* to the full, the reader needs to know that Désiré Nisard was a critic hostile to Romanticism and much scorned by Baudelaire, Gautier and others.[3] So, this pungent last phrase of *La Fanfarlo* was in the nature of an 'in-joke'. The very fact that, in order to understand it, we need the benefit of critical apparatus, not merely to enrich but to ensure our comprehension of the ironic antiphrasis contained in 'cet honnête M. Nisard', serves to accentuate the distinction between the 'modern', in the sense of the ephemeral (as here) and elements of 'modernité', fleetingly beautiful and nevertheless lasting in their transience (as in certain parts of the second narrative sequence). Structurally, however, this ambiguous end anticipates analogous types of closure in *Le Spleen de Paris*. Also, as has been pointed out very pertinently by Nathaniel

---

[3] Although his election to the Académie française, in 1850, over the head of Alfred de Musset, did nothing to endear him to the former followers of the 'Jeunes-France', Désiré Nisard was a distinguished classical scholar, held important posts at the Ecole Normale Supérieure, rue d'Ulm, and was esteemed by the Parnassians. His specialist interest in Decadent Latinity, notably his *Etudes sur les poètes latins de la décadence* (1834), presents an unexpected analogy with the prefiguration, in La Fanfarlo as Dancer (I, 572), of the Salome image, so beloved of Flaubert, Gustave Moreau and, later, such masters of Decadence as Huysmans and Wilde. See also the account, by René Huyghe, of Baudelaire's preference for the later period of decadence in classical literature, as opposed to Delacroix's stricter adulation of Homer and Virgil: Huyghe further traces this 'latinité...déjà tout asiatisée' to *Le Jeune Enchanteur* (1846), a novella translated by Baudelaire (*15*, p.89).

Wing, it implicates the reader, since 'it clearly sets up an uneasy alignment of the reader's views with a critic hostile to Romanticism' (*12*, p.186). The reader is left to pirouette in a state of uncertainty and ambiguity.

2. La Fanfarlo: *duality inherent in the narrator's attitude towards his discourse*

In the sense that the central duality, inherent in the double narrative sequence of *La Fanfarlo*, represents the deflation of the ideal by the real and, conversely, the defiant disdain of the world by the *dandy* whose ideal is encapsulated in the phrase, 'vivre et dormir devant un miroir' (I, 678), Baudelaire's novella has rightly been seen as exemplifying many of the themes of Romantic Irony.[4] This irony in Samuel Cramer's relationship to external reality has a parallel in Baudelaire's relationship to his novella. Baudelaire uses a narrator, or pseudo-author to tell the tale. This narrator is, however, no passive mouth-piece: by means of his constantly shifting view, the dynamic of life is introduced into what would otherwise have been the simple recounting of a story and, in consequence, a further dimension is introduced into the work. Constantly distancing himself, in almost prophylactic self-irony, from 'le pauvre Samuel' (I, 554), the narrator will, at times, intervene to address the reader directly as 'vous'. At the beginning of the second paragraph of the novella, such reader-involvement is actively sought: 'Comment vous mettre au fait, et vous faire voir bien clair dans cette nature ténébreuse...?' (I, 553). This narrative mode is picked up again later, when the pseudo-author mockingly warns the reader not to be taken in by Samuel, with the admonition '...gardez-vous de croire qu'il fût incapable de connaître les sentiments vrais' (I, 554). Elsewhere, the narrator will intervene to express his agreement with the protagonist: 'Cramer haïssait profondément, et il avait, *selon moi*, parfaitement raison, les grandes lignes droites en matière d'appartements' (I, 576; italics

---

[4] See, notably, *6*, *9*, *12* and *13* (Ch. II). For more general works on the concept of irony, the following are particularly helpful: Vladimir Jankélévitch, *L'Ironie*, Paris: Flammarion, 1964; Wayne C. Booth, *A Rhetoric of Irony*, Chicago and London: University of Chicago Press, 1974; René Bourgeois, *L'Ironie romantique*, Grenoble: Presses Universitaires de Grenoble, 1974; D.C. Muecke, *The Compass of Irony*, London and New York: Methuen, 1969, 1980.

mine). Generally, however, the distinction between 'je' and 'il' is clearly evident. Furthermore, this 'je' is at times extended into the plural form, to give a presentation of Samuel as 'l'homme le plus faux...de nos amis' (I, 574), where the first-person plural has less of a distancing function than in the quasi-Stendhalian use of such locutions as 'notre homme' (I, 554, 574), 'notre poète' (I, 568), 'notre jeune roué' (I, 569). We are all implicated (protagonist, narrator, author and reader), when the role of 'nous' widens out from the specific to the general, as in the use of 'nous' when applied to the non-achievement of Samuel in *Les Orfraies*, 'recueil de sonnets, comme nous en avons tous fait et tous lu' (I, 558). Yet, such authorial intrusions, intended to connote a critical attitude and a clearer sense of focus, are in no sense as rigorously objective as might at first appear, since the attitude of the narrator is coloured by his realization of the limitations of the protagonist. Ever conscious of the victim's confident unawareness, the ironical observer is never completely detached.

Just as, in the relationship between the first and the second narrative sequences, it was possible to establish a pattern of call and echo, a similar interplay may be detected between the narrative and the general discourse of the narrator. No doubt the most celebrated exemplification of this duality is the contrast between the narrator's initial description of Samuel (I, 553) and the ironically undercutting effect of the later descriptions of Samuel from the point of view of La Fanfarlo (I, 574): from being 'pur et noble', Samuel's forehead now appears 'trop haut'; the nose, which was earlier described as 'taquin et railleur', has been diminished to become a 'nez de priseur'; above all, the 'chevelure prétentieusement raphaélesque'[5] is now simply undisciplined ('cheveux en forêt vierge'). The regression, as C.A. Hackett suggests (*8*, p.320), is further accentuated by

[5] Cf. Baudelaire's blistering description of Millet's peasants as 'petits parias',with 'une *prétention* philosophique, mélancolique et *raphaélesque*' (*Le Salon de 1859*, II, 661; italics mine). It is clear that, in *La Fanfarlo*, Baudelaire enjoys giving contradictory accounts of Samuel's hair, described, before the first encounter with Mme de Cosmelly, as 'ses cheveux encrassés et emmêlés à l'excès' (I, 555). In a revealing note (I, 1417, n.3 to p.553), Claude Pichois suggests that, in this matter of Samuel's hair, Baudelaire may have been deliberately ironizing Balzac, the novelist whom he most admired.

the fact that the second of the two portraits has only three of the six features mentioned in the first one. Finally, the last nail in the coffin comes when La Fanfarlo, *despite* these features, which Samuel had no doubt seen as his glory, 'le trouva *presque* bien' (italics mine). The puncturing effect of this 'presque' (echoing two earlier though somewhat less devastating uses of the same effect (I, 571, 573)) may be compared with a similar technique adopted by Flaubert in *Madame Bovary*, where the coach 'ressembla *presque* à un tilbury' (italics mine). The ironical presentation of a superficially flattering portrait is thus further heightened, to the power of two, on its second appearance: the initial portrait had, after all, introduced the reader to Samuel, in terms of 'cette moitié de génie dont le ciel l'a doué', notable among all the 'demi-grands hommes' in Paris at the time.

A further instance of such regression in repetition may be seen in the 'doublet' of Samuel, as he emerges from meeting Mme de Cosmelly again in the Luxembourg Gardens (I, 557-58) and the subsequent account of how he fared later in life (I, 580). Having launched on his tirade against Walter Scott, 'l'ennuyeux écrivain', Samuel is ironically typed as belonging to 'la classe des gens *absorbants*' (I, 557): we are told that travelling salesmen are to 'poètes *absorbants*' as 'la réclame' is to 'la prédication', with this difference, that 'le vice de ces derniers est tout à fait désintéressé' (I, 558). Of the four 'livres de science' eventually written by Samuel, his volume on the four Evangelists takes up the theme of 'la prédication', while another, 'un mémoire sur un nouveau système d'annonces' (I, 580), echoes 'la réclame'.

Call and echo between the narrator's discourse and the narrative sequence, as such, are manifest in the account by Mme de Cosmelly of the favourable reports which attracted her to her future husband ('on citait de lui les traits les plus beaux: un bras cassé en duel pour un ami un peu poltron qui lui avait confié l'honneur de sa sœur, des sommes énormes prêtées à d'anciens camarades sans fortune' (I, 564)) and the ironical prefiguration of this in the narrator's description of the unpredictability of Samuel's behaviour: 'Il eût vendu ses chemises pour un homme qu'il connaissait à peine...Il se fût battu en duel pour un auteur ou un artiste mort depuis deux siècles' (I, 555). Again, the narrator's initial account of Samuel in terms of a 'dieu moderne et hermaphrodite' (I, 553) is echoed in the androgynous description of La Fanfarlo's leg (I, 572). Like Samuel, she too has long hair. Similarly, the presentation of La Fanfarlo as 'tour à tour décente, féerique, folle, enjouée' (I, 573) constitutes a union of incompatibles directly comparable to that indicated, at the outset, by the narrator in relation to Samuel.

All of these repetitions, ranging from internal contradictions (as in the case of the alternative descriptions of Samuel (I, 553; 574)) to variations on a theme (as in the androgynous parallels between Samuel and the Dancer), indicate a double level in the structure of *La Fanfarlo*, one of which relates to the world inside the double narrative sequence and the other to the world outside, the world of the narrator. For the reader, placed at a third point, outside this double helix, the effect of such conscious reordering of existing elements is essentially two-fold: firstly, these subtle changes of focus can produce rapier-like thrusts of irony, mirroring the non-achievement of the protagonist in both art and life; secondly, by the identification of certain constant elements, coupled with an awareness of the inherent paradox and contradiction endemic to human affairs, the reader becomes conscious of a harmony of opposites, between identification (static) and contradiction (dynamic), which lies at the heart of artistic illusion as presented by Baudelaire. Of the many literary avatars mentioned specifically in *La Fanfarlo*, perhaps Sterne (I, 554) and Diderot (I, 568) are the most significant in this connection. Coming after Sterne's anti-autobiography, *Tristram Shandy* (1760-67) and Diderot's anti-novel, *Jacques le fataliste* (1773), there is a case for viewing Baudelaire's *La Fanfarlo* as an anti-novella, at the end of what Albert George has described as the 'seed time of short narrative' (*23*, p.197) in French literature.

Indeed, *La Fanfarlo* subsumes a hidden roll-call of such literary avatars, each placed to produce maximum effect. Plagiarism is, of course, a noteworthy characteristic of Samuel: 'après une lecture passionnée d'un beau livre, sa conclusion involontaire était: voilà qui est assez beau pour être de moi! et de là à penser: c'est donc de moi, — il n'y a que l'espace d'un tiret' (I, 554). But plagiarism, coupled with irony, can provide the pretext for conscious innovation. Delacroix, in *Le Salon de 1846*, is, after all, portrayed as 'un des rares hommes qui restent originaux après avoir puisé à toutes les vraies sources' (II, 432). Later, in *Le Salon de 1859*, Baudelaire will declare: 'l'imitation est le vertige des esprits souples et brillants, et souvent même une preuve de supériorité' (II, 658).

By common agreement (see *20*, pp.42-49), Balzac is the major source of literary inspiration in *La Fanfarlo*: 'C'est Balzac traduit en Baudelaire par Baudelaire' (*4*, p.97). The debt to *La Fille aux yeux d'or* is indicated by Baudelaire in a footnote (I, 578) and the thematic resemblance to *Béatrix* is virtually textual (see *3*, pp.25-27). Beyond the multiple superficial parallels between a Rubempré or a Rastignac and Samuel Cramer in this 'terrible vie parisienne' (I, 553) (where even Mme de Cosmelly's address, 'dans une des rues les plus aristocratiques du faubourg Saint-Germain' (I, 558) shows the Balzacian imprint), themes are echoed, not merely to show the connection, but also to indicate points of difference. The most thinly-veiled quotation without quotation-marks in *La Fanfarlo* is the reference to Rastignac's 'coup d'oeil de vainqueur sur la ville maudite' (I, 574) at the end of *Le Père Goriot*, but with the ironical difference that Samuel does not muse over his triumph from a distance, but hastens to enjoy 'les diverses félicités qu'il avait à côté de lui'. Baudelaire rushes to the end of his narrative in a temporal acceleration which is not without counterpart in the world of Balzac. Conversely, however, as Jean Prévost (*20*, pp.44-46) and Claude Pichois (*3*, p.32) have indicated, Baudelaire leaves obvious gaps in his narrative, notably in relation to the breaking-off of the liaison between La Fanfarlo and M. de Cosmelly, which Balzac would not have omitted. Likewise, Baudelaire does little to inform the reader about the material and financial situation of the Cosmelly couple or about how Samuel came to have his newspaper articles published, whereas Balzac would have revelled in such details. Indeed, from many points of view, *La Fanfarlo* could be said to represent a reversal of Balzacian values (see *21*, p.219), in the sense that this arrival of a provincial young man in Paris ends in a bourgeois degradation of a kind which anticipates Flaubert as much as it echoes Balzac.

It would be tedious, and beyond the terms of reference of this short study, to go into all the literary quotations contained in *La Fanfarlo*, from Marivaux (I, 569), Laclos (I, 579),[6] Hoffmann (I, 554) (see *17*, pp.93-94), Musset (I, 561-62; 569-70), Pétrus Borel (I, 577) and Gautier (I, 576-77), to the tradition of *Tartuffe* (I, 568, 569; see *19*, pp.137-38, 143-44), with its repercussions on the theme of hypocrisy as treated by Stendhal. Virtually all of these echoes have been adopted and adapted by Baudelaire, with open-ended irony. Just as the identification of La Fanfarlo proceeds through metamorphoses in various national cultures (I, 573, 574), so Samuel is situated among his literary precursors in autobiographical or semi-autobiographical fiction. Imitation can give rise to parody, as happened with the gradual deflation of the stereotype of ill-fated Romantic genius. In Mme de Cosmelly, we have 'la discrète et vertueuse épouse' (I, 568) of the nineteenth-century personal novel. The difficulties involved in the attainment of Samuel's original ambition are almost visualized in the phrase which tells us that she was 'plus escarpée qu'elle n'en avait l'air' (I, 569), suggesting the hard climb up from the typically Romantic 'abîme'. She sees that she may have lost her husband's love by showing him 'trop d'amour' (I, 566), a theme common in the personal novel since *La Princesse de Clèves*, though here used by Baudelaire with ironic effect. Whatever Samuel's intentions may be, Mme de Cosmelly, as the reader can easily see, in advance of Samuel, will want to maintain their relationship on a footing of 'amitié' and 'choses platoniques' (I, 569). For his part, Samuel presents a parodying pastiche of his counterparts in the tradition

---

[6] But see C.A. Hackett's perspicacious comment, in relation to the parallel between this incident and that in Letter 47 of *Les Liaisons dangereuses*: 'Unlike Valmont, [Samuel] is never master of the situation, and he receives almost passively the news of his defeat' (*8*, p.324, n.11). See also *20*, p.44, for an alternative source for this incident, this time in the work of Balzac.

of the personal novel,[7] in that he is a conscious victim of paralyzing self-analysis (I, 560) and of his own 'impuissance' (I, 553).

The reworking of these literary themes constitutes a homage to a collective tradition and a flouting of this same tradition as an anachronistic irrelevance. Nowhere is this more evident than in the passage where the narrator feigns withdrawal from the narrative and, inspired by a quotation from Diderot (I, 568), taunts the reader with being too incredulous, seeking for verisimilitude where it is clear that intrigue, as such, is of quite secondary importance (cf. I, 556 and I, 579).

From the macrocontext to the microcontext, the same holds true, in relation to fossilized phrases, maxims and clichés. The impudent epigraph, *Aura sacra fames* (I, 580) (in a foreign language, like 'Any where out of the world' in *Le Spleen de Paris*), signifies, ostensibly, the cursed lust for gold. In context, however, it is cheeky in the extreme, since it indicates that the gratuitous gesture of literary creativity has degenerated, in the case of Samuel, into the money-making cultivation of functional practical writing on unmentionable subjects. Even the celebrated condemnation, 'dans le temps où nous avions le jugement si court et les cheveux si longs' (I, 558), has now been shown (I, 1420, n.3 to p.558) to have its origin in a popular proverb, 'La femme est un animal à cheveux longs et à idées courtes', although its full ironical force in Baudelaire's novella comes from its contextual situation.

Maxims are half-hidden in *La Fanfarlo*, to an extent which only emerges fully after a parallel reading of the approximately contemporaneous *Choix de maximes consolantes sur l'amour* (1846), and in the light of Balzac's *Physiologie du mariage* (1829) and some of the later prose poems, such as 'Portraits de maîtresses' (cf.I, 565). La Fanfarlo, for instance, is described as 'une danseuse aussi bête que belle' (I, 566), in a doublet of the maxim, 'La bêtise est souvent l'ornement de la beauté' (I, 549). Again, the agoraphobic 'calèche basse et bien fermée' (I, 574),

---

[7] *La Fanfarlo*, in its turn, will inspire further parodying pastiches (see that by Gustave Moreau, aimed against Hector Berlioz, discussed by Barbara Wright, 'A propos d'une page de Baudelaire: Gustave Moreau et Hector Berlioz', *Studi Francesi*, XVII, 3 (1973), pp.465-70).

which transports Samuel and La Fanfarlo to her house, where the small, low-ceilinged bedroom provides an idyllic 'réduit amoureux' (I, 578), is subsumed in a maxim-like generalization: 'Les sentiments intimes ne se recueillent à loisir que dans un espace très étroit' (I, 576). Conversely, the national stereotypes (with shades of Montesquieu, Mme de Staël and Stendhal), of which Samuel is presented as being 'le produit contradictoire' (I, 553), emerge clearly, in the *Choix de maximes consolantes sur l'amour*, as the 'Homme du Nord', enjoined to love 'femmes froides' and the 'Homme du Midi', more suited to 'les femmes ardentes' (I, 547).

The element of duality already indicated in relation to the double narrative sequence and, subsequently, in relation to the ambiguity inherent in the narrator's discourse and the narrative as an entity in itself, is most evident of all in the two dimensions which may be perceived in Baudelaire's use of language in *La Fanfarlo*: the outward form of the language, on the one hand and, on the other, the inner meaning which it subtends. Sometimes this 'double register' is conveyed by syntactical devices, such as the use of an adjective in anteposition, forming part of a chiasmus designed to produce a subtle contrast: 'féconde en desseins difficiles et en risibles avortements' (I, 553). Elsewhere, irony is expressed obliquely, but all the more effectively, through the medium of imagery: parodying the analogous collection of sonnets by Rubempré in *Illusions perdues* (*Les Marguerites*) and Baudelaire's own projected antecedents to *Les Fleurs du Mal* (*Les Lesbiennes*, later to become *Les Limbes*), Samuel entitles his collection *Les Orfraies*, referring, in the osprey, to a species of birds of prey, 'vilains oiseaux' (I, 559); the osprey here represents a negative form of bird (see *3*, p.57, n.2), or 'anti-oiseau' (see *25*, p.31), and the abortive inspiration thus suggested is further reinforced by the juxtaposition with a correspondingly negative term, 'mort-nés' (I, 560), in this context of non-achievement.

By far the most effective device for the ironizing of empty rhetoric is, however, as Michael Riffaterre has pertinently pointed out (*24*), Baudelaire's use of the cliché (see II, 609). Here, the 'double register' works quite devastatingly to show identity, in the shape of a well-worn cliché, coupled with contrast, in the sudden change or adaptation of one of the terms of the cliché. One of the examples selected by Michael Riffaterre for analysis in this connection is the hyperbolic reference to Samuel's 'voix tonnante' (I, 577), in calling after Flore not to forget La Fanfarlo's rouge, when fetching her costume. This fossilized cliché takes its effect from the incongruity of an excessively booming voice in the restricted confines of the dancer's small and low bedroom. Here, then, it is the context which renews the impact of the cliché. Elsewhere, the simple addition of 'romantique' to the well-worn expression, 'bavarder comme une pie' (I, 572), produces the requisite shock. The combination of cliché and metaphor is evident in the phrase, 'autres linges sales de la vie privée' (I, 571). Most frequently, however, it is the ironical intrusion of a phrase, hardened by use, into a context in which it would normally be considered alien, which constitutes the central innovative effect of Baudelaire's use of the cliché. Thus, the juxtaposition of 'paroles mielleuses' (I, 579) and the deflatory 'etc.' (cf.I, 569) permits of a widening of the semantic field.

If, then, we take the reworking of a proverb (e.g. 'dans le temps où nous avions le jugement si court et les cheveux si longs' (I, 558)), a self-quotation,[8] or a direct quotation (as already discussed in relation to Balzac and others), this 'double register', at the level of the microcontext, may be seen to produce an effect analogous to the principle of juxtaposition and discontinuity already established at the level of the macrocontext. 'Il faut remarquer', writes Baudelaire, in *De l'essence du rire*, 'que chaque terme de chaque classification peut se compléter et se nuancer par l'adjonction d'un terme d'une autre, comme la loi grammaticale nous enseigne à modifier le substantif par l'adjectif' (II, 536-37). One final example may serve to illustrate this point. 'Il n'est pas de rêve', Samuel tells Mme de Cosmelly, 'quelque idéal qu'il soit, qu'on ne retrouve avec un poupard glouton suspendu au sein' (I, 561).

[8] See, for example, I, 1421, n.3 to p.560; I, 1425, n.2 to p.574. Using previous work, published or unpublished, was common with Baudelaire. In this connection, Jules Mouquet's edition of Baudelaire's *Vers latins* (Paris: Mercure de France, 1933) is of particular interest.

This image is one which involves cross-referencing within *La Fanfarlo* (Samuel thinks of pregnancy as 'une maladie d'araignée' (I, 577), where the spider connotes imprisonment as well as enlargement) and self-quotation.[9] It also, as Michael Riffaterre has pointed out (*25*, p.57), constitutes a binary combination of polar opposites, in that 'poupard glouton' suggests a negative version of the stereotype of motherhood. The Romantic irony of the entire novella may be seen, in concentrated form, in the functioning of this combination of contradictory elements, rendered dynamic, not by any notation of external reality, nor yet again by any injection of strength from the plot (from which it is, strictly speaking, extraneous), but simply by its negativity, suggesting much of the rich, ironic potential of the authorial persona of Baudelaire.

* * * * *

In the light of the multiple dualities already discussed, the three apparently self-contained sections in the second narrative sequence would need to be up-graded from the status of digressions, which 'ruined the economy of the tale', in the words of Albert George (*23*, p.207), to a position of prime importance in any assessment of the originality and achievement of Baudelaire in *La Fanfarlo*. These three sections, on dance, the culinary arts and architecture respectively, constitute a mosaic-type pattern.

These ostensibly parenthetical passages[10] contribute to the narrative obliquely, as Nathaniel Wing has shown with great subtlety (*12*, pp.182-85). They do so on two levels. Firstly, Samuel, in his seduction of La Fanfarlo, was able to cultivate the detachment necessary to the Dandy and the true Artist. La

[9] Cf. 'les hideurs de la fécondité', in 'J'aime le souvenir de ces époques nues...' (first published in 1857, but the original date of composition of which is thought to be between 1841 and 1845? (*16*, p.357)). A parallel image will be taken up later, in 'Bohémiens en voyage' (1851), with reference to 'le trésor toujours prêt des mamelles pendantes'.

[10] The first passage is disarmingly introduced with the phrase, 'cela soit dit en passant' (I, 573); the second contains the distancing device inherent in 'Samuel avait coutume de dire' (I, 575); the third marks the direct intrusion of the 'moi' (I, 576) of the narrator and includes a lapidary maxim (I, 576).

Fanfarlo, for her part, transcends physical attractiveness and appeals to Samuel through a multiplicity of identities and aesthetic values, in the history of pantomime and the *commedia dell'arte* (Colombine, Zéphyrine (I, 573) etc.). 'Un battement perpétuel', in the words of Jean Starobinski, 'enlève le corps dans une signification fictive et le renvoie de cette signification à la présence physique littérale' (*26*, p.58). The Dancer is identified in the context of her culture ('un caprice de Shakespeare et une bouffonnerie italienne' (I, 574)), just as the Poet is situated in the context of his literary tradition. As Nathaniel Wing has put it, 'the consonance of the lovers' sentiments is only possible because they have renounced the *myth of presence*' (*12*, p.182). La Fanfarlo prefigures the section 'La Femme' in *Le Peintre de la vie moderne*, in that, amid the magic, glitter and fantasy of the theatre, 'la femme et...la robe' constitute 'une toilette indivisible' (II, 714). Her make-up (a further prefiguration of 'Eloge du maquillage') combines with her spangled costume to form part of her attraction for Samuel, just as the connivance of the glance, in 'A une passante', is inseparable from the swirl of the dress. Furthermore, her aesthetic control of movement and form is comparable to the blend of 'volupté' and 'connaissance', so central to artistic achievement, in the view of Baudelaire. The reference to the 'grands peuples voluptueux et savants' (I, 576), in the context of architecture, is thus in keeping with the combination of passion and order in the sequence as a whole. The culinary arts, we are told, require a vigorous understanding of the chemical properties of matter, consciously selected with a view to inducing a sense of well-being or voluptuousness. La Fanfarlo has so far transcended mastery of technique as a ballet-dancer that she has become 'sublime dans son art, autant comédienne par les jambes que danseuse par les yeux' (I, 573). When once she loses this domination, the charm is broken: La Fanfarlo becomes a high-class tart ('une espèce de lorette ministérielle'[11]) and gets fat. 'La femme est le contraire du Dandy', Baudelaire

---

[11] Cf. Baudelaire's comments on the 'création' of the 'lorette' by Gavarni, in *Quelques caricaturistes français* (II, 560). The term is generally thought to stem from the proximity of Notre-Dame-de-Lorette in what was one of the main quarters where artists lived in nineteenth-century Paris.

will comment later, in *Mon Cœur mis à nu* (I, 677). 'Donc elle doit faire horreur'. A similar fate awaits Samuel when he becomes the victim of his own passion, loses his sense of artistic detachment and drops, in consequence, from the status of Poet-Dandy: 'Il avait souvent singé la passion; il fut contraint de la connaître;...ce fut...l'amour maladif des courtisanes' (I, 579-80). Baudelaire's interest in dance anticipates subsequent developments in the work of Mallarmé and Valéry, coupled with manifestations of the Salome figure in the work of Flaubert, Gustave Moreau, Huysmans and Wilde.

The second level on which these parenthetical passages advance the narrative obliquely lies in the extent to which La Fanfarlo, the Dancer, may be seen as a disguised self-projection of Samuel, the Poet. Not only does she present an emblem with a double aspect (aesthetic, as well as physical; controlled, as well as seductive); she also presents a manifestation of the age-old distinction between self and anti-self, face and mask, which was to be of such fascination for the mirror-contemplating Samuel. Musset's Fantasio embodies just such a disguised self-representation. In the case of Baudelaire, however, the effect is almost one of *mise en abyme* in that Samuel, already semi-autobiographical, here gives a projection of the Dancer as the consummate artist he himself vainly hopes to become, a projection given heightened irony by the narrator's distinctly anti-establishment thrusts in the closing paragraphs of the novella. In the transition from mythological goddesses to a real ballerina; in the metamorphosis of a genre scene to 'ce ravissant taudis, qui tenait à la fois du mauvais lieu et du sanctuaire' (I, 576), with echoes, besides, of Delacroix's *Femmes d'Alger*, as described by Baudelaire in *Le Salon de 1846* (II, 440); in the shift of emphasis from a non-genius, an anti-hero, to an ideal of beauty explicable in terms of 'modernité', or the encapsulation of the ephemeral; in all of these ways, Baudelaire is introducing a new dimension into his novella and is producing an effect which is strikingly original. Far from giving a direct narrative account of the relationship between the Poet and the Dancer, he suggests this evolution obliquely through a discussion of the consonance of their views (corresponding closely, of course, with his own). The parallel sets develop in almost geometrical progression, with the truffle acting as an intensifier (see *12*, p.184): 'la truffe...a l'effet de plusieurs zéros après un chiffre' (I, 575).

The Poet/Dancer sequence of *La Fanfarlo* is written in poetic prose. It aims at combining the unexpected and the predictable in a metrical prose best typified by the description of the Dancer's movements, 'pleins d'une cadence précise' (I, 574). In general terms, however, rhythm is seen by Baudelaire as incompatible with prose writing, 'un obstacle insurmontable à ce développement minutieux de pensées et d'expressions qui a pour objet la *vérité*' (II, 329-30). These aesthetic considerations may well have been a major factor in the non-fulfilment of Baudelaire's early ambition, as expressed by him in a letter to his mother in 1847 (*5*, I, p.145), to become a successful novelist, and repeated in 1858 (*5*, I, p.451), after the publication of *Les Fleurs du Mal*. The 'multitude de tons' (II, 330), which he admired in relation to Poe's short stories, coupled with the unity of effect which he saw as ideal for that art form (II, 329), were well exemplified by Baudelaire in *La Fanfarlo*. But this work is an anti-novella in a context more particularized than that of literary history: it did nothing to discourage Baudelaire from including *contes* in *Le Spleen de Paris*; yet, by his evident lack of interest in plot and sequential analysis, it may well have convinced the poet that his qualities were not those which he deemed appropriate for a successful novelist. On the other hand, the sequences in the novella which, superficially, appear to be only tangential to the story-line, are those in which Baudelaire's achievement is most noteworthy, in terms of suggestive art. The 'entente profonde', between the Poet and the Dancer, is expressed 'dans chaque regard et dans chaque parole' (I, 576), a typically Baudelairean communion of 'l'esprit' and 'les sens'. Their conversation is characterized as being 'tantôt brutale comme un chiffre, tantôt délicate et parfumée comme une fleur ou un sachet' (I, 576), a combination of the precise and the subtly evocative. Perhaps the most lasting impression of *La Fanfarlo* is just such a tension between the message and the medium through which it is conveyed. All the various dualities then converge in the ultimate communion between the author, in his multiple transformations, and the reader, whose response is actively sought. Where such a symbiosis can be achieved, the highest value of creative art, as posited by Baudelaire, has been attained.

Select Bibliography

I EDITIONS OF WORKS BY BAUDELAIRE

1   *Œuvres complètes*, ed. Claude Pichois, 2 vols, Paris: Gallimard,
    Bibliothèque de la Pléiade, 1975-76.
2   *La Fanfarlo*, ed. Jules Mouquet, Paris: A. Tallone, Edition du
    centenaire, 1945.
3   *La Fanfarlo*, ed. Claude Pichois, Monaco: Editions du Rocher, 1957.
4   *La Fanfarlo*, ed. Yves Florenne, Nice: La Diane française, 1969.
5   *Correspondance*, ed. Claude Pichois & Jean Ziegler, 2 vols, Paris:
    Gallimard, Bibliothèque de la Pléiade, 1973.

II CRITICISM ON LA FANFARLO

6   Ferran, André, 'Baudelaire juge de Baudelaire', *Revue d'Histoire
    Littéraire de la France*, XXXVI, 3 (juillet/septembre 1929), pp.447-57.
7   Galand, René, '*La Fanfarlo*', in *Baudelaire: poétiques et poésie*, Paris:
    Nizet, 1969, pp.232-47.
8   Hackett, C.A., 'Baudelaire and Samuel Cramer', *Australian Journal of
    French Studies*, VI, 2-3 (1969), pp.317-25.
9   Heck, Francis S., 'Baudelaire's *La Fanfarlo*: an example of Romantic
    irony', *The French Review*, XLIX, 3 (February 1976), pp.328-36.
10 Jeremy, John, 'Samuel Cramer—Eclectic or Individualist?', *Nottingham
    French Studies*, XX, 1 (1981), pp.10-21.
11 Pichois, Claude, 'Autour de *La Fanfarlo*: Baudelaire, Balzac et Marie
    Daubrun', *Mercure de France*, 328 (décembre 1956), pp.604-36.
12 Wing, Nathaniel, 'The Poetics of Irony in Baudelaire's *La Fanfarlo*',
    Neophilologus, LIX, 2 (April 1975), pp.165-89.

III GENERAL WORKS OF CRITICISM ON BAUDELAIRE, TO WHICH
REFERENCE IS MADE

13 Blin, Georges, *Baudelaire*, Paris: Gallimard, 1939.
14 Butor, Michel, *Histoire extraordinaire: essai sur un rêve de Baudelaire*,
    Paris: Gallimard, 1961.

15 Huyghe, René, 'Le Poète à l'école du peintre', in Baudelaire: *OEuvres complètes*, ed. Albert Demazière, Paris: Editions de Saint-Clair, 1974, pp.87-93.

16 Leakey, F.W., *Baudelaire and Nature*, Manchester University Press, 1965.

17 Lloyd, Rosemary, *Baudelaire et Hoffmann: affinités et influences*, Cambridge University Press, 1979.

18 Pichois, Claude, 'Le Demi-frère du poète des *Fleurs du Mal*: Alphonse Baudelaire ou le magistrat imprudent', in *Baudelaire: études et témoignages*, nouvelle édition revue et augmentée, Neuchâtel: A la Baconnière, 1967, pp.44-58.

19 Pommier, Jean, *Dans les chemins de Baudelaire*, Paris: Corti, 1945.

20 Prévost, Jean, *Baudelaire: essai sur l'inspiration et la création poétiques*, Paris: Mercure de France, 1953.

21 Ruff, Marcel, *L'Esprit du mal et l'esthétique baudelairienne*, Paris: Colin, 1955; Geneva: Slatkine Reprints, 1972.

22 Ziegler, Jean, 'Emile Deroy (1820-1846) et l'esthétique de Baudelaire', *Gazette des Beaux-Arts*, LXXXVII (1976), pp.153-60.

IV OTHER WORKS

23 George, Albert J., *Short Fiction in France: 1800-1850*, Syracuse University Press, 1964.

24 Riffaterre, Michael, *Essais de stylistique structurale*, Paris: Flammarion, 1971.

25 ——, *La Production du texte*, Paris: Seuil, 1979.

26 Starobinski, Jean, *Portrait de l'artiste en saltimbanque*, Geneva: Skira, Les Sentiers de la création, 1970.

Note: At the time of going to press, the author wishes to add her recommendation of the recent article by Bernard Howells, 'Baudelaire: Portrait of the Artist in 1846', *French Studies*, XXXVII, 4 (Oct. 1983), 426-39.

Le Spleen de Paris

1. Early nineteenth-century orientations in the prose poem

Unlike their late eighteenth- or early nineteenth-century contemporaries in England and Germany, the first generation French Romantics and their pre-Romantic forbears were essentially writers in *prose*.[1] This was not necessarily, however, for want of a theoretical understanding of the scope and potential of poetry in verse. Both Rousseau, in his *Essai sur l'origine des langues* (1761), and Mme de Staël in *De l'Allemagne* (1810)[2], for example, show a remarkable awareness in principle of poetry's possibilities but both were also aware that the sterility of the eighteenth-century French poetic tradition, with its excessive reliance on classical or pseudo-classical models, presented the potential lyric poet with almost insurmountable difficulties. Rousseau wrote in his *Confessions*: 'J'ai fait de temps en temps quelques médiocres vers; c'est un exercice assez bon pour se rompre aux inversions élégantes et apprendre à mieux écrire en prose; mais je n'ai jamais trouvé dans la poésie française assez d'attrait pour m'y livrer tout à fait'[3]; and for Mme de Staël much of the motivation for writing *De l'Allemagne* lay in the conviction that French literature — and particularly poetry — could be saved from paralysis only by rejuvenation at foreign sources.

Since in the period 1770-1820 the most vital strands of lyricism in France were *not* to find their expression in verse, it was natural that the poetic potential of prose should be explored. The following famous passage from the fifth *Promenade* of Rousseau's *Les Rêveries du promeneur solitaire* (published in 1782), for example, anticipates not only the psychological mood

---

[1] For fuller details of the origin and history of the French prose poem and poetic prose see *23*, pp.9-19; *32*, pp.19-49; *33*, pp.viii-xii; and *34*, pp.13-206.

[2] Especially chs.IX and X of the First Part (see ed. S. Balayé, Paris: Garnier-Flammarion, 1968, vol. I, pp.197-209).

[3] See ed. M.Launay (Paris: Garnier-Flammarion, 1964), vol.I, p.195.

but also the poetic style of the nineteenth-century prose poem:

> Quand le soir approchait je descendais des cimes de l'île et
> j'allais volontiers m'asseoir au bord du lac, sur la grève,
> dans quelque asile caché; là le bruit des vagues et
> l'agitation de l'eau fixant mes sens et chassant de mon âme
> toute autre agitation la plongeaient dans une rêverie
> délicieuse où la nuit me surprenait souvent sans que je
> m'en fusse aperçu. Le flux et le reflux de cette eau, son
> bruit continu mais renflé par intervalles frappant sans
> relâche mon oreille et mes yeux, suppléaient aux
> mouvements internes que la rêverie éteignait en moi et
> suffisaient pour me faire sentir avec plaisir mon existence,
> sans prendre la peine de penser. De temps à autre naissait
> quelque faible réflexion sur l'instabilité des choses de ce
> monde dont la surface des eaux m'offrait l'image: mais
> bientôt ces impressions légères s'effaçaient dans
> l'uniformité du mouvement continu qui me berçait, et qui
> sans aucun concours actif de mon âme ne laissait pas de
> m'attacher au point qu'appelé par l'heure et par le signal
> convenu je ne pouvais m'arracher de là sans effort.[4]

Here in Rousseau, as later in Chateaubriand, the writer's
absorption into a certain type of environment finds natural
expression in a poetic prose that was nearing the realization of
what Baudelaire was later to define in his preface to *Le Spleen de
Paris* as: 'le miracle d'une prose poétique, musicale sans rythme
et sans rime, assez souple et assez heurtée pour s'adapter aux
mouvements lyriques de l'âme, aux ondulations de la rêverie,
aux soubresauts de la conscience' (I, 275-76). In, for example,
the following passage from Chateaubriand's *Itinéraire de Paris à
Jérusalem* (1811), a spell-bound response to a setting analogous
to that evoked by Rousseau gives rise to a prose similarly supple
in its expression of 'mouvements de l'âme' and 'ondulations de
la rêverie' — to the extent that, in the two passages, the
'soubresauts de la conscience' are expressed in identical terms:
'Je ne pouvais m'arracher de là sans effort' (Rousseau); 'Je ne

[4] See ed. J.Voisine (Paris: Garnier-Flammarion, 1964), p.100.

pouvais m'arracher à ce spectacle' (Chateaubriand).[5]

> Je ne pouvais m'arracher à ce spectacle: quelles pensées n'inspire point la vue de ces côtes désertes de la Grèce, où l'on n'entend que l'éternel sifflement du mistral et le gémissement des flots! Quelques coups de canon que le capitan-pacha faisait tirer de loin à loin contre les rochers des Maniotes, interrompaient seuls ces tristes bruits par un bruit plus triste encore: on n'apercevait sur toute l'étendue de la mer que la flotte de ce chef des Barbares: elle me rappelait le souvenir de ces pirates américains qui plantaient leur drapeau sanglant sur une terre inconnue, en prenant possession d'un pays enchanté au nom de la servitude et de la mort; ou plutôt je croyais voir les vaisseaux d'Alaric s'éloigner de la Grèce en cendres, en emportant la dépouille des temples, les trophées d'Olympie, et les statues brisées de la Liberté et des Arts.[6]

Rousseau and Chateaubriand thus provided a source not only of Romantic themes but also, more specifically, a model for a certain kind of poetic prose. When, therefore, Albert Chérel describes the workings of Chateaubriand's prose in the following manner, what he says could equally well be applied to the style of a prose poet of the next generation such as Maurice de Guérin:

> un rythme ralenti, lorsqu'il espace les syllabes accentuées, ou que par leur alternance habile avec les syllabes sourdes, il sait prolonger leur durée: ainsi — et par l'immobilité alanguie ou rigide qu'il donne alors à ses images — il paraît s'immobiliser lui-même à contempler sa séduction de peintre. Ailleurs, ou presque en même temps, le rythme s'accélère pour évoquer le désordre d'un orage, ou les fiévreuses amertumes du "cœur de l'homme"; encore est-

[5] Such terms are used by Baudelaire himself in a similar situation in 'Déjà': 'Semblable à un prêtre à qui on arracherait sa divinité, je ne pouvais, sans une navrante amertume, me détacher de cette mer si monstrueusement séduisante...'

[6] Ed. J. Mourot (Paris: Garnier-Flammarion, 1968), pp.71-72.

il que dans ces passages de brusquerie, l'accent de paix ou
de complaisance a le dernier mot. (*34*, p.200)

The special achievement of Maurice de Guérin (1810-39) in *Le
Centaure* and *La Bacchante* (both completed, it is believed, in
1836)[7] was the imposition of *formal* unity on the poetic prose
style that had been perfected by Romantic and pre-Romantic
writers such as Chateaubriand and Rousseau. For in Guérin's
prose poems, lyricism — the expression through poetic language
of an emotional response to an object, person or experience — is
not as it mostly was with his predecessors an occasional
phenomenon but an essential and dynamic part of the total
fabric of the work. *Le Centaure* exemplifies this process not only
in the way the choice of the central myth allows thematic
elements constantly to integrate themselves into one another,
but also in the way the formal features organize themselves in
such a way as to create a feeling of aesthetic unity. By
systematizing the kind of procedure Chérel, in the passage
above, notes in the context of Chateaubriand, Guérin succeeds
in *immobilizing* his paragraphs at their point of closure (very
often round some central but static image) enabling them thus to
attain to an almost strophic kind of unity — as in the last
paragraph of *Le Centaure*:

> Pour moi, ô Mélampe! je décline dans la vieillesse,
> calme comme le coucher des constellations. Je garde
> encore assez de hardiesse pour gagner le haut des rochers
> où je m'attarde, soit à considérer les nuages sauvages et
> inquiets, soit à voir venir de l'horizon les hyades
> pluvieuses, les pléiades ou le grand Orion; mais je
> reconnais que je me réduis et me perds rapidement comme
> une neige flottant sur les eaux, et que prochainement j'irai
> me mêler aux fleuves qui coulent dans le vaste sein de la
> terre.[8]

[7] See Maurice de Guérin: *Pages choisies* (ed. D. Secretan, Manchester:
University Press, 1965), pp.xix-xx.

[8] Ibid., p.8. For further discussion of this passage, see David H.T. Scott,
'Maurice de Guérin's *Le Centaure*: an allegory of the operations of poetic
prose', *French Studies Bulletin*, 2 (Spring 1982), pp.3-6.

A complex interweaving of formal and thematic motifs takes place in *Le Centaure* not only within each passage but also from paragraph to paragraph, with the result that these latter, operating as a series of interconnected cycles, through tension and interrelation, are able to create a feeling of aesthetic unity. Thus, whereas a poet in verse might have used rhyme to produce a dynamic that was simultaneously progressive and retrospective, Guérin is able to create similar effects using altogether less tangible means. For it is the prose rhythms themselves which, in conjunction with a careful placing and repetition of key images, create the effect of unity yet complexity, the consistent presence of which is essential if we are to feel that what we are reading is a *poem*.

The deceleration of prose's linear energies, the immobilizing or fixing of the text or fragment of text so that poetic values may be released, will become a major preoccupation of prose poets after Guérin: but we see it already in the work of his contemporary Aloysius Bertrand (1807-41).

'C'est en feuilletant pour la vingtième fois au moins, le fameux *Gaspard de la Nuit*, d'Aloysius Bertrand ... que l'idée m'est venue de tenter quelque chose d'analogue ...', Baudelaire wrote in the dedicatory preface to those of his prose poems published in *La Presse* in 1862. Although, as he himself pointed out (and as we shall later see), his achievement in the prose poem was very different from that of Bertrand, it was the author of *Gaspard de la Nuit*, rather than Maurice de Guérin, who opened his eyes to the potential of the *poème en prose*. Whereas the length and narrative style of *Le Centaure* make it, as Bernard has pointed out, something of a 'cas limite' (*32*, p.79) within the genre and thus much less susceptible to imitation or successful adaptation, the opposite was true of the poems in Bertrand's *Gaspard de la Nuit*, the consistent brevity and economy of means of which were an invaluable example to later prose poets.

The subtitle of *Gaspard de la Nuit* — *Fantaisies à la manière de Rembrandt et de Callot* — gives as much insight into the poems' formal structure as into their typical themes, for in seeking a fresh way of shaping the short prose text, Bertrand turned to the visual arts and adapted from them a manner of organizing images that was both compact and painterly. Instead therefore of developing his themes and motifs within a broad narrative or descriptive structure, Bertrand, like the artist, organizes the various aspects of his text into a primarily *aesthetic* pattern within the given limits of the page, the blank margins of which will 'frame' the various elements of the composition.

Bertrand was able to achieve this transposition of graphic techniques into linguistic expression by inventing or adapting formal units the chief function of which would be the 'squaring' or immobilizing of the text. The typical format of the poems in *Gaspard de la Nuit* is thus that of five, six or seven well-spaced couplets organized beneath one or two epigraphs. From couplet to couplet clusters of images are juxtaposed with the minimum of narrative[9] or syntactical *enjambement* from one formal unit to the next. The spaces between the couplets decelerate syntactical as well as rhythmic energies and contrive to impose upon each couplet a stanza-like unity. By slowing down the rhythm and linear, logical impulses of prose, by isolating his figures and images within couplets themselves framed by the page, Bertrand succeeds, in a manner different from but analogous to that of Guérin, in channelling the endlessly flowing stream of language into a state of relative immobility and reflective calm.

The interest of *Le Livre du promeneur*[10] of Jules Lefèvre-Deumier (1797-1857) is not as intrinsic as that of *Le Centaure* or *Gaspard de la Nuit* but the 366 'pièces en prose' which constitute it are worth noting in that they show a nineteenth-century French writer immediately before (and almost certainly known to) Baudelaire experimenting with the possibilities of the short, poetic text in prose in a manner which, superficially at least, appears to have more in common with Baudelaire's practice in this form than did the earlier and more original achievements of Guérin and Bertrand. Lefèvre-Deumier seemed to be less

[9] Or if there is narrative development, its temporal unfolding is radically telescoped; see the Max Milner edition of *Gaspard de la Nuit* (Coll. Poésie, Paris: Gallimard, 1980), pp.34-35.

[10] Quotations from this work will be from the first edition, published in Paris by Amyot, 1854.

concerned than Guérin with establishing a marked and individual prose style and, unlike Bertrand, did not consistently adhere to the same types of formal structure. His approach to the wide range of subjects tackled in *Le Livre du promeneur* varies considerably and although alexandrines and other fragments of verse poetry are to be found scattered through it — as in the opening phrase of 'Un Souvenir':

Le lac était tranquille, la nuit pure et limpide.
Tout dormait dans les airs...

or at the end of 'Le Passé', the final phrase of which, shaved of a syllable, might have appeared as the last line of a sonnet by Heredia:

Mill(e) nageurs silencieux qui sont les souvenirs

—these features remain accidental and sporadic; they are not, as they are with Guérin, incorporated into a formal design.

A more consistent feature of Lefèvre-Deumier's prose texts in *Le Livre du promeneur* is the way in which the shift from general to specific, from the object to its interpretation, is effected through the mechanism of analogy.[11] This is, of course, a convention well established in mid-nineteenth-century poetry — particularly amongst Parnassian poets (Heredia, Leconte de Lisle) and those on the Parnassian fringe (Gautier, Baudelaire, Houssaye, Lefébure and the early Mallarmé) and one which is consistently applied as a structural principle in the Parnassian sonnet, the bipartite form (octave/sestet) of which lends itself particularly well to the creation of metaphorical transformations.[12] This tendency is discernible in Lefèvre-Deumier's verse poetry (as is shown, for example, in his sonnet 'La Colombe poignardée'), but it is interesting to see how it also

[11] Fragments of a theory of metaphor are to be found scattered through *Le Livre du promeneur*, for example, in 'Les Comparaisons', 'La Peau de serpent', 'L'Eclipse', etc.

[12] See David H.T. Scott, *Sonnet Theory and Practice in Nineteenth-Century France: Sonnets on the Sonnet* (Publications of the University of Hull, 1977), pp. 56-59.

becomes a structural feature of many of Lefèvre-Deumier's
short prose pieces. It offers a means of diverting the linear and
logical energies of prose downwards, converting a horizontal,
discursive language into one that is vertical or metaphorical.
There are many examples of this procedure in *Le Livre du
promeneur* but of particular interest is 'Voyage autour du
monde' in which we find a process later to be developed by
Baudelaire in his prose poem 'L'Invitation au voyage':

> Mon vaisseau n'a besoin, pour faire le tour du globe, ni de
> rames, ni de voiles, ni de roues tournées par la vapeur.
> Mon vaisseau, c'est ma pensée...

This search through metaphor for the infinite in the finite, the
impalpable captured in the commonplace object, naturally leads
Lefèvre-Deumier to cultivate images and themes to which,
though common to Romantic poets, Baudelaire was to give
particularly distinctive development. Thus, when writing on
Time (as in 'Un Souvenir', 'Le Passé', 'Les Horloges', 'Le
Sablier', 'Le Fleuve', 'La Nostalgie') or the Voyage (as in
'Voyage autour du monde', 'Le Navire gelé', 'Le Pays des
heureux', 'Le Vaisseau', 'La Plus Belle Contrée', 'L'Orient',
'La Vraie Patrie'), Lefèvre-Deumier's titles read like an
anticipatory repertory of Baudelairian themes.

Unlike those of Baudelaire, however, Lefèvre-Deumier's
images are mostly generalized. The process of metaphorical
conversion through which the object becomes metaphor is a
mechanical one: there is a tedious inevitability about the way
that Lefèvre-Deumier's chosen images become symbols for the
thoughts or spirit of the poet. Although, as we have seen,
Lefèvre-Deumier develops many themes subsequently exploited
by Baudelaire, he seldom manages to create a feeling of tension
or excitement that might rejuvenate the potential of a
commonplace or hackneyed idea. Perhaps one of the reasons for
this is that, unlike the sceptical and provocative Baudelaire,
Lefèvre-Deumier is an essentially superficial and conservative
thinker. A deist epicurean, he recommends faith ('La Foi') not
doubt, political docility and obedience ('La Royauté') not

revolt, and manages to reduce to bathos a theme as potentially exciting as the exotic voyage; thus the answer to the intriguing question posed in 'La Plus Belle Contrée':

> Connaissez-vous le plus beau pays de la terre: un pays où l'on ne regrette les plantes d'aucun climat, et dont on regretterait les paquerettes dans les champs de roses de cachemire...?

is not El Dorado or 'un pays de Cocagne' evoked in the manner of Baudelaire but 'ta patrie'.

Although Lefèvre-Deumier is, like Baudelaire, concerned with exploring the evocative potential of symbols, he is, in practice, too hasty and sententious in the interpretation of his images: he does not leave them much life of their own and they thus remain essentially *prosaic*. Occasionally he does refrain from interfering with or too readily interpreting his images and on these occasions we feel premonitions of Baudelaire *poète en prose*. The exclamation in 'Un Conseil', for example:

> Que de combinaisons capricieuses et charmantes, que d'éclat dans les nues!

strikingly anticipates the final confession in Baudelaire's 'L'Etranger', but more often, with Lefèvre-Deumier, the text's closure is effected glibly and aphoristically. The moral or philosophical *pointe* rather than the suggestive image becomes the *raison d'être* of the text, reducing its status to that of an epigram or abortive essay rather than a *poème en prose*. This is a risk, of course, that Baudelaire, as we shall see, will also run in *Le Spleen de Paris*, in which he is moralist as often as poet. But Baudelaire's 'morality' is the result of deep and revelatory self-interrogation, not, as with Lefèvre-Deumier, a system largely constructed with conventional elements imported from outside.

The aim of this short excursion into the history of the prose poem before Baudelaire has been, firstly, briefly to sketch in the general context from which *Le Spleen de Paris* was to emerge; and, secondly, in showing what Baudelaire's nineteenth-century forerunners had made of the new genre, to reveal its remarkably diverse potentialities at this time. For Baudelaire's originality as a prose poet, as will be seen, lies essentially in his success, while he profits from their example, in creating forms very different from those of his predecessors.

2. Le Spleen de Paris: *general considerations*

(i) *Introduction*

As had been the case with *Les Fleurs du Mal*,[13] Baudelaire was for a long time undecided about the title that would best suit his prose poems, formulae as diverse as *Poëmes nocturnes*, *Poèmes en prose*, *Le Promeneur solitaire*, *Le Rôdeur parisien*, *La Lueur et la fumée*, *Petits Poèmes en prose*, *Le Spleen de Paris* and *Petits Poèmes lycanthropes* all having been suggested or used (in that order, though with some *reprises*) between 1857 and 1866.[14] To a considerable extent, the way one reads Baudelaire's prose poems will depend on the title one chooses to consider them under, the two more definitive of the various options (that is, the ones most consistently used by Baudelaire in the later stages of his prose poems' development) — *Le Spleen de Paris* and *Petits Poèmes en prose* — suggesting markedly different emphases or intentions. The various editors of Baudelaire the prose poet have, depending on their angle of approach, opted for one or other of the two titles. Robert Kopp in the standard critical edition of Baudelaire's prose poems, selects *Petits Poëmes en prose* but does not argue very convincingly for this choice (2, pp. lxv-lxvi), whereas the case for *Le Spleen de Paris* has been put altogether more cogently and persuasively by Claude Pichois (I, 1298-1301). Meanwhile, Henri Lemaitre and Marcel Ruff both hedge their bets by entitling their popular editions: *Petits Poèmes en prose (Le Spleen de Paris)*.

Le Spleen de Paris (the title consistently used in this study when referring to Baudelaire's prose poems) would seem to be the more appropriate title. In the first place, *Petits Poèmes en prose* seems to define a *genre* as much as suggest a title and the

[13] For the evolution of this collection's title, see I, 791-97.

[14] For fuller details of the evolution of Baudelaire's prose poems, see 4, pp.xiii-xiv and I, 1298-99.

definition it proposes is somewhat problematic since the question of whether all the texts grouped under this heading are in fact prose poems is an open one.[15] Partisans of the *Petits Poèmes en prose* school may, of course, retort with Kopp that '*Le Spleen de Paris* s'accorde mal à la vérité d'un recueil dont la majorité des pièces ne sont pas spécifiquement parisiennes' (*2*, p.lxv). This argument appears to weaken, however, if one concedes that the poems do not actually have to be *about* Paris to merit inclusion under the title *Le Spleen de Paris*. As Pichois succinctly puts it: '*Le Spleen de Paris* est un recueil de poèmes en prose marqué par un esprit parisien; dans les sentiments se reflète une âme parisienne et moderne, les sujets fussent-ils étrangers à Paris ou même exotiques' (I, 1300).

In the second place, however, it is the emphasis on the concept of 'Spleen' (to be taken, as Pichois notes, in its widest possible sense and which I would see as englobing states or responses ranging from melancholy to ill humour aggressively asserted) that really tips the balance in favour of *Le Spleen de Paris* as title: it not only reflects the markedly splenetic tone of the work (a characteristic it shares with Baudelaire's later works in general, whether the *Journaux intimes* or *Pauvre Belgique*) but also differentiates it from the more consistently idealistic emphasis of *Les Fleurs du Mal* in which 'Spleen' and 'Idéal' exist in a relationship of tension but also of balance. Whereas in *Les Fleurs du Mal* many of the poems (and these are amongst Baudelaire's greatest works) are memorable for their triumphant lyricism (that is, their ability, through their suggestive and evocative language, to heighten and transform the possibilities of experience), this is seldom the case with the later prose texts. *Le Spleen de Paris* thus seems to be the most appropriate title for a formally problematic but tonally consistent work and it will be primarily from this point of view that it will be considered in the pages that follow.

Unlike Guérin or Bertrand, Baudelaire was not primarily or fundamentally a *poète en prose*. His prose poetry is only one aspect of a much vaster *œuvre* which included art and literary

[15] The problem of classifying Baudelaire's prose poems — both generically and thematically — will be dealt with later in this study.

criticism, translation, *Les Paradis artificiels* and the *Journaux intimes*, not to mention *Les Fleurs du Mal*; if any one text dominates the others, it is of course the last which, quite apart from its intrinsic merits, has had an influence on subsequent developments in French literature that has been greater than that of all Baudelaire's other works combined. Whereas a poet such as Rimbaud was, from 1873, to abandon his earlier efforts in verse poetry to commit himself exclusively to the *poème en prose*, for Baudelaire *Le Spleen de Paris* had essentially been envisaged as a complement to *Les Fleurs du Mal*. Some of Baudelaire's best poems in verse were written concurrently with the prose texts of *Le Spleen de Paris*, that is, in the early 1860s. That Baudelaire did not in any way see these latter as superseding the verse poetry is made clear in this extract from a letter to Victor Hugo of 1863: 'Je me propose de vous envoyer prochainement *Les Fleurs du Mal* (encore augmentées) avec *Le Spleen de Paris*, destiné à leur servir de pendant' (*30*, II, p.339).

Baudelaire's prose poems do not then, as has often misleadingly been suggested — by, for example, Bernard (*32*, p.111) and Kopp (*2*, pp.xxvi-xxvii) — represent simply an attempt to escape from the 'limitations' imposed by verse. On the contrary, versification, far from being an obstacle to freedom of expression, was seen by Baudelaire as being a valuable source of creative inspiration. As he confirms in the *Salon de 1859* (that is, two years after some of his early prose poems, under the title of *Poëmes nocturnes*, had appeared in *Le Présent*):

il est évident que les rhétoriques et les prosodies ne sont pas des tyrannies inventées arbitrairement, mais une collection de règles réclamées par l'organisation même de l'être spirituel. Et jamais les prosodies et les rhétoriques n'ont empêché l'originalité de se produire distinctement. Le contraire, à savoir qu'elles ont aidé l'éclosion de l'originalité, serait infiniment plus vrai. (II, 626-27)

And later in the same work, writing of the dangers of the *genre fantastique* in painting, Baudelaire, significantly, compares it to poetry in prose:

> C'est dans ce genre surtout qu'il faut choisir avec sévérité; car la fantaisie est d'autant plus dangereuse qu'elle est plus facile et plus ouverte; dangereuse comme la poésie en prose, comme le roman, elle ressemble à l'amour qu'inspire une prostituée et tombe bien vite dans la puérilité ou dans la bassesse; dangereuse comme toute liberté absolue. (II, 644)

The equation 'modernité'/'poésie en prose' has also been somewhat overstated by commentators. Bernard's thesis, for example, leads her to develop this superficially seductive idea in an oversimplified and tendentious manner. She argues, for example, that 'seule une prose très souple et dégagée de toute contrainte formelle … pourra épouser sans durcissement les palpitations de la vie, les fluctuations du sentiment au sein d'une grande cité' (*32*, pp. 109-10). Bernard does not however say why this should be so or demonstrate her point by confronting two of Baudelaire's later 'urban' texts, one in prose, one in verse, and thus providing the expressive superiority of the former. One is led to ask: Are the 'Tableaux parisiens' of *Les Fleurs du Mal* less modern and authentic than their prose equivalents in *Le Spleen de Paris* simply because they are in verse? And one wonders if it would be possible to find in Baudelaire's prose poetry any phrases which capture more perfectly the fluctuations and complexities of the modern psyche as it attempts to adjust itself to an urban environment than the following lines from 'Le Cygne':

> Andromaque, je pense à vous! Ce petit fleuve,
> Pauvre et triste miroir où jadis resplendit
> L'immense majesté de vos douleurs de veuve,
> Ce Simoïs menteur qui par vos pleurs grandit,
>
> A fécondé soudain ma mémoire fertile
> Comme je traversais le nouveau Carrousel...

or

> Paris change! mais rien dans ma mélancolie
> N'a bougé! palais neufs, échafaudages, blocs,
> Vieux faubourgs, tout pour moi devient allégorie,
> Et mes chers souvenirs sont plus lourds que des rocs...

Baudelaire does, of course, say in the much cited preface to the prose poems:

> Quel est celui de nous qui n'a pas, dans ses jours d'ambition, rêvé le miracle d'une prose poétique, musicale sans rythme et sans rime, assez souple et assez heurtée pour s'adapter aux mouvements lyriques de l'âme, aux ondulations de la rêverie, aux soubresauts de la conscience?

and goes on to affirm that

> C'est surtout de la fréquentation des villes énormes, c'est du croisement de leurs innombrables rapports que naît cet idéal obsédant. (I, 275-76)

It is nevertheless an oversimplification to assume without question that *Le Spleen de Paris* in fact realizes the dreamed-of 'miracle' or discovers a language more expressive than that of Baudelairian verse. In the first place, what Baudelaire defines in his preface as a 'prose poétique, musicale', is a style which relatively few of his prose poems adopt throughout; and those in which an attempt towards this style is clearly being made (such as 'Le Crépuscule du soir', 'Un Hémisphère dans une chevelure', 'L'Invitation au voyage') are often very close to verse poems of similar title or theme in *Les Fleurs du Mal*. Secondly, Baudelaire's definition of this ideal 'prose poétique' seems to imply an extended and *continuous* style of writing which, whilst rendering his formula irresistibly quotable in the context of the poetic prose of writers such as Chateaubriand or Guérin, makes it seem, paradoxically, much less applicable to many of his own prose poems. These latter, either because of their relative shortness or because the more developed of them (such as 'Une Mort héroïque', 'Le Joueur généreux', 'La Corde', etc.) adopt a more consistently narrative and *prosaic* style, may not always seem to offer a particularly apt illustration of Baudelaire's ideal conception of prose poetry.

Observations such as these make it important, when considering the nature and originality of *Le Spleen de Paris*, to ignore neither the problematic nature of the relationship between Baudelairian theory and practice of the prose poem nor the complexity of the links — more fundamental and elaborate than might at first appear — between the prose poems and Baudelaire's other works.

(ii) *'Le Spleen de Paris' in the wider context of Baudelaire's works*

Although the intention of producing an entire volume of prose poems was not expressed in writing by Baudelaire until 1857 (see *30*, I, p.395) — the year in which *Les Fleurs du Mal* was first published — he seems to have had some notion of the possibilities of prose poetry almost from the beginning of his literary career. Already in *La Fanfarlo*, the hero, Samuel Cramer, is described as converting into prose 'quelques mauvaises stances composées dans sa première manière' (I, 560) while, as commentators have noted (see *8*, pp.18-19, and Barbara Wright, above, p.15), various parts of the text of *La Fanfarlo* itself are in fact prose 'transpositions' of poems or fragments of poems in verse composed, in all probability, by Baudelaire himself (see *2*, pp.xxxii-xxxv).

A close connection between prose text and prior or contemporary poem in verse is also to be discerned in Baudelaire's first published prose poems proper, two of which appeared in 1855, followed by six in *Le Présent* of 1857 (see *2*, pp. 419-22) under the following titles: 'Le Crépuscule du soir', 'La Solitude', 'Les Projets', 'L'Horloge', 'La Chevelure' and 'L'Invitation au voyage'. Three of these texts in particular (the first and the last two) seem to suggest that Baudelaire's early prose poems were outgrowths of his poetry in verse (although the prose version of 'La Chevelure' was in fact first published two years before the one in verse). This tendency is also evident in the nine pieces published in *La Revue fantaisiste* of 1861 in which, of the three previously unpublished prose poems included, one — 'Les Veuves' — shares a similar theme with the poem in verse 'Les Petites Vieilles', first published in 1859.

After 1861, however, the connection between prose and verse texts becomes markedly more tenuous. The prose poems which will later form the bulk of *Le Spleen de Paris* and which began to appear in reviews from 1862 onwards (*4*, pp.i-xvii) seem to reflect a fresh orientation in Baudelaire's development of the prose poem, one which seemed to be moving away from *Les Fleurs du Mal* and towards preoccupations evident in other Baudelairian works of the 1860s. Two important questions are thus raised: Why did Baudelaire abandon his early approach to the prose poem which seems to have been much influenced by his preoccupations as author of *Les Fleurs du Mal*? What was the nature of the reorientation in Baudelaire's prose poetry of the 1860s and how does it relate to his other, non-poetic, works of the period?

Let us deal with the former question first. In his first prose poems, Baudelaire chose, naturally enough, to concentrate on those themes which had shown themselves, in his verse, to be most susceptible to *poetic* development; themes, that is, which lent themselves to elaboration in terms of images and through sensuous and imaginative association ('horizontal' and 'vertical' correspondences) rather than through logical or narrative links. But the question here is: How well did these themes — themes of enormous poetic potential — adapt themselves to treatment in prose? To a certain extent the answer to this question must remain a matter of opinion, but if we are to base our judgement on the Baudelairian prose poem's overall development it would seem that, from Baudelaire's point of view at least, the early prose 'translations' of texts in verse did not achieve the results he was seeking, since after about 1861, as we have noted, he largely abandoned this approach to the prose poem. A comparison of prose and verse versions of a similar theme or set of images provides possible reasons for Baudelaire's change of tack.

'Un Hémisphère dans une chevelure' and 'L'Invitation au voyage', for example, both illustrate the dangers of a *prose poétique* in which liberties derived from poetry have not been accompanied by disciplines sought at the same source. Both poems develop in a series of short prose paragraphs a highly suggestive theme — *chevelure, voyage* — but one in which the images' potential, without the more abstract harmonizing and ordering disciplines of verse line and stanza, they are not always able fully to exploit. It is important to note here that the poems in verse ('Parfum exotique' and 'La Chevelure'; 'L'Invitation au voyage') from which the two prose texts in question are believed to derive, far from being 'mauvaises stances', distinguish themselves by the complexity of their formal structure. One, 'Parfum exotique', is a regular sonnet in which an already complex rhyme-scheme is complicated further by a choice of rhymes in the sestet which becomes progressively richer (*climats, mâts, marine, tamariniers, narine, mariniers*). The function of this accumulation of rhyme within rhyme, is calculated to recreate in *formal* terms the synaesthetic process that is the subject of the poem in which, as it develops, sensations — olfactory, visual, aural — are seen to be perceived *within* sensations, images embedded in further images, giving rise to that synthesis of 'vertical' and 'horizontal' *correspondances* which the Baudelairian poem typically set out to achieve. A contrasting formal solution had been sought by Baudelaire in 'La Chevelure', in which the discipline of the regular four-line stanza in alternating rhymes is given an extra expressive dimension by the inclusion of a fifth line between, as it were, lines 3 and 4. Thus a scheme in *abab* is replaced by one in *abaab*. The effect of this is to disturb the logical, symmetrical balance of the quatrain and to create a sensation of swaying and over-reaching which is marvellously expressive of both the lyrical striving of the poet and the maritime context from which he derives his most important images. Meanwhile, in 'L'Invitation au voyage', Baudelaire developed a stanzaic structure of different complexity. In this poem, three twelve-line stanzas, in each of which single heptasyllabic lines alternate with pentasyllabic couplets, are interspersed with a refrain, also a couplet, but this time heptasyllabic, the serene but paradoxical message of which, through successive repetitions, takes on a hypnotic, incantatory power.

These examples show how Baudelaire, a great master of the *strophe* (one might argue on the basis of *Les Fleurs du Mal* — half of which take the form of the sonnet — that Baudelaire *thought* in stanzas), when tackling themes of immense suggestiveness, was careful to elaborate for them a commensurately complex formal orchestration. It is, after all, the function of form to generate dynamism, to structure and extend thematic developments. It is precisely a lack of dynamism of this sort in Baudelaire's prose versions of poems which sometimes leads the latter to stagnate: denied the shorthand of juxtaposition or cross-reference through rhyme, lacking the rhythmic dynamism and immense scope for variation offered by the verse line, they are sometimes left to spread out their thematic wares in what seems a more arbitrary manner. Compare, for example, the random inventory which opens the last paragraph of the prose version of 'L'Invitation au voyage':

Ces trésors, ces meubles, ce luxe, cet ordre, ces parfums,
ces fleurs miraculeuses, c'est toi. C'est encore toi, ces
grands fleuves et ces canaux tranquilles...

with its altogether tauter and more efficient verse equivalent:

Là, tout n'est qu'ordre et beauté,
Luxe, calme et volupté.

Furthermore, the relative lack of scope for formal variation leads Baudelaire to amplify thematic elements: 'gargoulettes' and 'pots de fleurs' ('Un Hémisphère dans une chevelure'), black tulips and blue dahlias ('L'Invitation au voyage') further clutter texts already dangerously overloaded with images many of which seem purely decorative.

On the other hand, ideas that remain implicit or more purely

suggestive in the poems in verse are often made, in the prose
texts, altogether more explicit, the result of which is sometimes a
curious defusing of a metaphor's potential. Thus the languorous
rhetorical question that brings 'La Chevelure' to such a fitting
close:

> N'est-tu pas l'oasis où je rêve et la gourde
> Où je hume à longs traits le vin du souvenir?

is replaced, in the prose poem, by a somewhat clumsy handling
of a similar analogy:

> Quand je mordille tes cheveux élastiques et rebelles, il me
> semble que je mange des souvenirs.

For Bernard (*32*, p.142), this more literalized and 'prosaic'
treatment of an analogy, which had shocked some nineteenth-
century contemporaries of Baudelaire (see the article 'Causerie'
by Pierre Véron in *Le Journal amusant* of 11 October, 1862,
cited in *2*, pp.lv-lvi), was a much more original and authentic
expedient than that of the verse. For Barbara Johnson (*19*,
pp.464-65), on the other hand, it is an example of the way some
of Baudelaire's prose poems undermine, through excessively
literalizing, the metaphorical developments of the verse poems
from which they derive. (This thesis is also elaborated on in
Johnson's *Défigurations du langage poétique*, see *18*, pp.
31-55.)

Formal agents such as rhythm and rhyme are not, of course,
the only guarantees of lyrical (as opposed to logical or narrative)
dynamism in literary works: as Guérin's *Le Centaure* and certain
passages in Baudelaire's early prose poems themselves show,
there is also such a thing as a dynamism of images. But,
paradoxically, for some temperaments, images are more likely
to link themselves vitally or expressively if they are submitted to
a process of abstraction rather than elaboration. *Le Centaure*,
for example, is characterized by the relative banality of its basic
images but this does not matter since their poetic effect depends
on the subtle variation and overlaying of their implications.

Mallarmé was later to become the greatest master of this technique — both in prose and verse — but Baudelaire (whose images, incidentally, supplied Mallarmé with more than enough material for a lifetime's refinement) was also aware of the potential of this approach. Thus, at the end of the prose version of 'L'Invitation au voyage', by concentrating on the development of one essential image — that of the ship setting sail — and by incorporating its elaboration into a formal structure both rhythmically and syntactically symmetrical, Baudelaire produces a fragment of prose that perfectly expresses the poetic circularity of the experience:

> Ces énormes navires qu'ils charrient, tout chargés de richesses, et d'où montent les chants monotones de la manœuvre, ce sont mes pensées qui dorment ou qui roulent sur ton sein. Tu les conduis doucement vers la mer qui est l'Infini, tout en réfléchissant les profondeurs du ciel dans la limpidité de ta belle âme; — et quand, fatigués par la houle et gorgés des produits de l'Orient, ils rentrent au port natal, ce sont encore mes pensées enrichies qui reviennent de l'Infini vers toi.

Nevertheless, the lesson Baudelaire seems to have learned from his prose poems of the 1850s was that, firstly, it was, on the whole, pointless to try to compete with verse poetry on its own ground and, secondly, that certain themes and images were much more susceptible of extended elaboration in verse than in prose. Furthermore, there was always the risk that those prose poems which attempted to develop the kinds of themes that were already part of the stock of Baudelairian or more generally Romantic lyricism might appear to be no more than prose transpositions of pre-existing poems or, alternatively, merely raw material for a future poem in verse. As Baudelaire remarked in a letter to Arsène Houssaye in December 1861: '...vous avez fait aussi quelques tentatives de ce genre, et vous savez combien c'est difficile particulièrement pour éviter de montrer le plan d'une chose à mettre en vers' (*30*, II, p.207). In order to make of the prose poem something more than a pale imitation or parody of *Les Fleurs du Mal*, Baudelaire was thus led to seek out a fresh approach to the genre. Let us now turn to the second question posed at the beginning of this section and explore the implications of Baudelaire's change of strategy both in the specific context of *Le Spleen de Paris* and also in the wider one of his other works of the period.

The two decades of Baudelaire's life as a creative writer (from the early 1840s to the mid 1860s) seem to give expression to three fundamental vocations: those of poet, critic and moralist. These three orientations are however, though distinct, seldom totally isolated from one another in Baudelaire's work. Baudelaire was never a pure aesthete; one of the chief characteristics of his work is that it should manifest a close interweaving of the various essential facets of his personality. The truth of the following statement from 'L'Ecole païenne' is thus of particular relevance to Baudelaire:

toute littérature qui se refuse à marcher fraternellement entre la science et la philosophie est une littérature homicide et suicide. (II, 49)

Hence, works as apparently different as *Les Paradis artificiels* and the *Salons* (especially those of 1846 and 1859) have profound implications for Baudelaire the poet as well as for Baudelaire the moralist and art critic; *Les Fleurs du Mal*, itself, represents a great imaginative synthesis in which Baudelaire the moralist and art critic as well as Baudelaire the poet find expression. What is remarkable about Baudelaire's major literary enterprises of the 1860s, however (*Pauvre Belgique* and the *Journaux intimes* as well as *Le Spleen de Paris*), is that they tend to give freer scope to one particular vocation — that of *moralist* — more than to the other two (I use the word 'moralist' here above all in the French sense of *moraliste*, investigator of human psychology). Charles Mauron, in *Le Dernier Baudelaire*, notes for example that in *Fusées* and *Mon Cœur mis à nu* (which, combined, form the *Journaux intimes*), 'presque huit sur dix de ces notations appartiennent au moi social. Elles formulent des jugements philosophiques ou moraux, expriment des convictions, prennent parti' (*22*, p.138). Mauron goes on to indicate the close connection between Baudelaire's preoccupations in the *Journaux intimes* and *Le Spleen de Paris* showing how, in the latter work, 'le rêve trop chargé de colère, se décharge mieux dans les opinions d'un carnet que dans des poèmes travaillés' (*22*, p.140). And Baudelaire himself describes the poet of *Le Spleen de Paris*, in a letter to Sainte-Beuve,[16] as 'un nouveau Joseph Delorme accrochant sa pensée rapsodique à chaque accident de sa flânerie et tirant de chaque objet une morale désagréable' (*30*, p.583).

The implications of this for Baudelaire's prose poems in generical terms is that the *moral* truth with which the later Baudelaire becomes increasingly concerned will seek a form of expression which, as one might expect, is different from that sought by the lyric poet. It is thus to the more *prosaic* forms of *conte*, *essai* and *épigramme* that Baudelaire *moraliste* will increasingly turn in the prose poems written after 1861, and the series of twenty *Petits Poèmes en prose* published by *La Presse* in three different issues in 1862 bears striking witness to this new development.

In this series, texts such as 'Le Désespoir de la vieille', 'Un Plaisant', 'Le Chien et le flacon', 'Le Mauvais Vitrier', 'A une heure du matin', 'La Femme sauvage et la petite-maîtresse', 'Le Vieux Saltimbanque', 'Le Gâteau', 'Le Joujou du pauvre' and 'Les Dons des fées' (which constitute by far the larger proportion of Baudelaire's previously unpublished prose poems at this time), show how the balance is already being tipped from lyricism towards the pole of morality, particularly in the sense that the prose poems seem increasingly to create dynamism and impact less through a vivid juxtaposition of images than through the dramatisation or confrontation of moral or philosophical dilemmas. Some of the moral preoccupations manifest in the texts just cited do, of course, still find expression in

[16] Sainte-Beuve's *Vie, poésie et pensées de Joseph Delorme* (1829) was, for its time, original not only in its intimate, contemporary, even *prosaic* style but also for the way in which it attempted to show (a favourite thesis of Sainte-Beuve) the close links between the creative work and life and thought of a writer. Baudelaire saw his prose poems as being analogous to those of Sainte-Beuve in verse in that *Le Spleen de Paris* very much represented the 'vie, poésie et pensées' of the later Baudelaire.

contemporary Baudelairian verse: thus, 'A une heure du matin'
reveals a moral self-examination similar to that of 'La Fin de la
journée' (published in the second edition of *Les Fleurs du Mal*,
in 1861) or 'L'Examen de minuit' (published in *Le Boulevard*, in
1863) whilst texts such as 'La Femme sauvage et la petite-
maîtresse' (to be followed by 'Le Galant Tireur'[17]) recall
Baudelaire's intermittently sadistic attitude towards the loved
woman expressed with corrosive elegance in poems such as 'Une
Charogne' (published in the first edition of *Les Fleurs du Mal*, in
1857). The fact that *Les Fleurs du Mal* give almost as rich
expression to Baudelaire the moralist (and art critic) as to
Baudelaire the poet, has already been emphasized. What
distinguishes the prose texts published from 1862 onwards,
however, is the altogether more consistent and explicit nature of
their moral interpretations and their prosaic style. 'Le Joujou du
pauvre', for example, is an adaptation of part of a much longer
essay — *Morale du joujou* — published in *Le Monde littéraire* in
1853, but one in which, in spite of considerable reworking,[18] the
somewhat unnecessary *emphase* of the final phrase:

> Et les deux enfants se riaient l'un à l'autre frater-
> nellement, avec des dents d'une *égale* blancheur

still presses home its moral in a decidedly prosaic manner.
Meanwhile, even those texts in the 1862 series which start with
bursts of lyrical energy — such as 'La Chambre double':

> Une chambre qui ressemble à une rêverie, une chambre
> véritablement *spirituelle*, où l'atmosphère stagnante est
> légèrement teintée de rose et de bleu...

or 'Le *Confiteor* de l'artiste':

> Que les fins de journées d'automne sont pénétrantes!

[17] An early outline of this, interestingly, is to be found in Baudelaire's *Fusées*
(see *2*, p.336).

[18] For fuller details (and a different assessment) of this, see *2*, pp.260-62, and
32, p.116.

Ah! pénétrantes jusqu'à la douleur!

begin to shift their concern from poetic to moral or philosophical truth. Thus 'La Chambre double' ends with the following assertion:

Oui! le Temps règne; il a repris sa brutale dictature. Et il me pousse, comme si j'étais un bœuf, avec son double aiguillon. — "Et hue donc! bourrique! Sue donc, esclave! Vis donc, damné!"

whilst the lyricism which opened 'Le *Confiteor* de l'artiste' is superseded by an altogether more philosophical style, the poem closing on the following *pointe*:

L'Etude du beau est un duel où l'artiste crie de frayeur avant d'être vaincu.

The effect of this general trend in Baudelaire's later writing — and particularly on his prose poems — was to push poetry very much towards the margins of Baudelairian experience and expression. The result was that, instead of his lyricism being given the extended and richly orchestrated treatment so characteristic of his poetry in verse of the 1850s, it finds expression in altogether briefer and more fragmentary texts (of which, as we shall see, 'L'Etranger' is the type *par excellence*). Baudelaire's predicament was thus by the early 1860s not unlike that of the hypothetical poet he describes in his article 'Théophile Gautier' published in *La Revue fantaisiste* at about this time (15 July 1861, though the following extract also appeared in an earlier article on Poe of 1857):

Je dis que si le poète a poursuivi un but moral, il a diminué sa force poétique; et il n'est pas imprudent de parier que son œuvre sera mauvaise. La poésie ne peut pas, sous peine de mort ou de déchéance, s'assimiler à la science ou à la morale; elle n'a pas la Vérité pour objet, elle n'a qu'Elle-même. Les modes de démonstration de vérité sont autres et sont ailleurs. La Vérité n'a rien à faire avec les chansons. (II, 113)

The manner in which this passage appears exactly to contradict
the one written by Baudelaire ten years earlier in 1852 (cited
above, p.58) is worthy of comment since the two passages seem
to illustrate the fundamental polarity of Baudelaire's thought on
art. Whereas it was Baudelaire *moraliste* speaking in 1852 (that
is, at a time when the *art for art's sake* movement was at its
apogee, Gautier's *Emaux et camées* being published that year) it
was, paradoxically, on the threshold of completing his most
specifically 'moral' works that was to be heard the voice of
Baudelaire poet and aesthete in his celebration of that same
Gautier, Parnassian poet *par excellence* and the 'parfait
magicien ès lettres françaises' to whom *Les Fleurs du Mal* had
been dedicated. So we have here two instances of Baudelaire the
critic (the first passage is from the article 'L'Ecole païenne', the
second from one on Gautier) diagnosing and, perhaps,
attempting to correct, tendencies he recognizes in his own work
of the period. Seen in this light, the passage in the Gautier article
constitutes a particularly disturbing prognostic, since it predicts
a diminution of the poet's 'force poétique' and a corresponding
decline in the quality of his work if the moralist's path is too
single-mindedly followed. Baudelaire was, however, far too
skilful and complex a writer to succumb totally to the dangers he
foresaw with such clairvoyance and lucidity; although, as the
correspondence and journals of the 1860s show,[19] the risk of
'déchéance' and poetic sterility is a constantly imminent threat
to the author of *Le Spleen de Paris*, Baudelaire nevertheless
managed to salvage some brilliant fragments from his later
experience. How he did so and the particular originality of his
achievement will now be considered.

(iii) *The originality of 'Le Spleen de Paris'*

Baudelaire's aim in *Le Spleen de Paris* seems to have been not so

---

[19] We read, for example, in the *Journaux intimes* (I, 668): 'Maintenant j'ai
toujours le vertige, et aujourd'hui 23 janvier 1862, j'ai subi un singulier
avertissement, j'ai senti passer sur moi *le vent de l'aile de l'imbécillité.*'

much to create a poetic prose in the manner of Chateaubriand or Guérin as to explore what Georges Blin has described as 'la poésie d'un prosaïsme' (*11*, p.463), that is, the poetic potential of prose discovered, as it were, almost by accident[20] as it went about its everyday business. In the poem 'Le Soleil' (one of the 'Tableaux parisiens' section of *Les Fleurs du Mal*) Baudelaire had described how

> Le long du vieux faubourg, où pendent aux masures
> Les persiennes, abri des secrètes luxures,
> Quand le soleil cruel frappe à traits redoublés
> Sur la ville et les champs, sur les toits et les blés,
> Je vais m'exercer seul à ma fantasque escrime,
> Flairant dans tous les coins les hasards de la rime,
> Trébuchant sur les mots comme sur les pavés,
> Heurtant parfois des vers depuis longtemps rêvés.

In a similar way, later, the poet of *Le Spleen de Paris* will take both himself and his prose on exploratory walks. The 'rôdeur parisien' or 'promeneur solitaire' will seek from this programme of exercise not only a certain form of stylistic relaxation ('c'est encore *Les Fleurs du Mal*, mais avec *beaucoup plus de liberté*': *30*, II, p.615; italics mine), but also the discovery of fugitive poetic effects.

Now it was the 'everyday business' of Baudelaire's prose as it recorded his perceptions as moralist and art critic which was frequently to provide the poet with the fragments of poetry or poetic insight he was seeking. Art criticism in particular provided valuable exercise and discipline for Baudelaire's prose, necessitating the development of a style capable of combining vivid description with accurate analysis. Baudelaire had, of course, from the beginning of his career distinguished himself as an art critic: mention has already been made of the inspiration which the poet of *Les Fleurs du Mal* derived from his study of painting and the visual arts generally. But by the 1860s, more recent and innovatory artistic styles were at last beginning to explore that 'héroïsme de la vie moderne' which Baudelaire had,

[20] 'accrochant sa pensée rapsodique à chaque accident de sa flânerie' (II, 583).

in his *Salon de 1846*, already been urging contemporary artists to portray; the possibilities of the rapid sketch or incidental evocation of the essentially transitory or topical scene or event — as in the swift improvisations of Guys, the impressionism of Boudin, the urban modernism of Manet — presented themselves with a new vividness to Baudelaire's imagination and were to have a corresponding effect on his poetic preoccupations. Whereas, in *Les Fleurs du Mal*, the energies of Baudelaire the art critic and admirer of Delacroix and the Romantic school were to find an outlet in the elaboration of many *transposition d'art* poems, in his later writing, Baudelaire was to seek less consciously worked-out effects and, in doing so, evolved a prose style which was suitable for use by both art critic and poet alike.[21] It is thus not surprising to find that some fragments in Baudelaire's later writings on art (and in particular *Le Peintre de la vie moderne*) match passages in the prose poems. The evocation of Paris at twilight in the later prose version of 'Le Crépuscule du soir':

> Crépuscule, comme vous êtes doux et tendre! Les lueurs roses qui traînent encore à l'horizon comme l'agonie du jour sous l'oppression victorieuse de sa nuit, les feux des candélabres qui font des taches d'un rouge opaque sur les dernières gloires du couchant

may be closely linked to a similar evocation in *Le Peintre de la vie moderne* (published in 1863):

> Mais le soir est venu. C'est l'heure bizarre et douteuse où les rideaux du ciel se ferment, où les cités s'allument. Le gaz fait tache sur la pourpre du couchant. (II, 693)

The latter passage seems to be a more successful example of

---

[21] It is known that Baudelaire had, in 1860, intended to write a series of short prose texts to accompany Meryon's *Vues de Paris*. Owing, however, to a fundamental difference of opinion between the two artists over the aim of Baudelaire's contribution, nothing of the latter materialized. Furthermore, none of the prose poems which later constitute *Le Spleen de Paris* is directly inspired by Meryon.

Baudelaire's later prose style, avoiding the somewhat overblown rhetoric of the former passage and managing to juxtapose without embarrassment the striking trimeter: 'Le gaz fait tache sur la pourpre du couchant' with the more prosaic: 'Honnêtes ou déshonnêtes, raisonnables ou fous, les hommes se disent: "Enfin la journée est finie!" ' The discovery of a vein of poetry embedded in prose did not however solve the problems of the prose poet whose major concern was its extraction and establishment as an autonomous unity. Whereas a fragment of poetic prose could create a striking effect if it surged unexpectedly from a broader, more prosaic context (and this was one of the peculiar charms of the texts of Rousseau, Chateaubriand and Baudelaire the art critic), this striking effect was often partly a function of the *contrast* such a passage made with the surrounding text. To justify the existence of the fragment of poetic prose in its own right as a complete text in isolation was another and more difficult problem.

Baudelaire sought several ways out of this difficulty. In his early prose poems (such as 'Un Hémisphère dans une chevelure') he sought to replace the energy that in his poems in verse had been generated partly by the dynamism of their metrical and stanzaic forms by essentially rhetorical structures supported by a consistent use of repetition and syntactical parallelism. But, as we noted in the previous section of this chapter, these structures did not always provide sufficient discipline for the plethora of images which, linked by rhetorical or discursive means, very often had no *formal* function. It was only with Rimbaud that the radical solution to this problem was to be found, for the energy and unity of the short prose texts of the *Illuminations* were to be derived from the images themselves, the *dynamique* of which was as often created through pure juxtaposition as through repetition or syntactical parallelism.

The problem with Baudelaire here was that, as was suggested in the introduction to this section, he was primarily a *verse* poet: the richness of his most typical images' potential — *le crépuscule, la chevelure, le voyage* — demanded a formal concentration that prose as he understood it would seldom be able fully to provide. Baudelaire seems to have realized this since, in the early 1860s, he had begun to evolve a fresh strategy as prose poet and seek out alternative solutions to the problem of how to confer aesthetic autonomy on short prose texts. Baulking at the solution Rimbaud was later to adopt (Rimbaud's chief criticism of Baudelaire, it will be remembered, was that living in a 'milieu trop artiste', 'la forme si vantée en lui est mesquine: les inventions d'inconnu réclament des formes nouvelles'[22]), two alternatives remained open to Baudelaire. The first was simply to seek formal structures different from those provided by verse, ones which could be better adapted to providing dynamism and autonomy in prose texts. This was the easier and less original solution since these forms — which were in effect those of *essai*, *conte*, short story or anecdote — were ready-made and could be adapted to Baudelaire's purposes. (In fact the larger proportion of Baudelaire's later prose poems fall into the *essai/conte* category as the tables in the next chapter will show.) The second and much more interesting solution was that of *emphasizing* and *cultivating* the arbitrary and fragmentary nature of short prose texts which would not thus need to bolster up their fragile structure through other means (see *10*, pp. 152-53).

The fact that Baudelaire did not attempt a prose translation of his great poem of 1859, 'Le Voyage' (its conversion to prose in the manner of other Baudelairian prose poems of the later 1850s would not be difficult to imagine), is indicative of his desire to find a fresh solution to the problem I have outlined. When thus, in the mid-1860s, Baudelaire set out to adapt the voyage idea to the prose poem, the result was three altogether more oblique and fragmentary texts — 'Déjà' (1863), 'Le Port' (1864), and 'Any where out of the world' (1867) — all of which reflect different aspects of the voyage theme but none of which exudes that self-confident lyricism so typical of Baudelaire's verse poems of the 1850s of which 'Le Voyage' was one of the last great examples.

This apparent lack of poetic self-confidence and relative decline in lyrical energy was to become a characteristic of Baudelaire's prose poems of the 1860s which, like waning stars,

[22] 'Lettre du voyant', *Œuvres* (ed. S. Bernard, Paris: Garnier, 1960), p.349.

transmitted their poetic messages as feeble and distant glimmers or in sudden and self-destructive explosions. Whereas in the last stanzas of 'Le Voyage' the poem's stately lyricism is brought to an imposing and memorable climax:

> O Mort, vieux capitaine, il est temps! levons l'ancre!
> Ce pays nous ennuie, ô Mort! Appareillons!
> Si le ciel et la mer sont noirs comme de l'encre
> Nos cœurs que tu connais sont remplis de rayons!
>
> Verse-nous ton poison pour qu'il nous réconforte!
> Nous voulons, tant ce feu nous brûle le cerveau,
> Plonger au fond du gouffre, Enfer ou Ciel qu'importe?
> Au fond de l'inconnu pour trouver du *nouveau*!

'Le Port' closes with the most languorous of gestures:

> Et puis, surtout, il y a une sorte de plaisir mystérieux et aristocratique pour celui qui n'a plus ni curiosité ni ambition, à contempler, couché dans le belvédère ou accoudé sur le môle, tous ces mouvements de ceux qui partent et de ceux qui reviennent, de ceux qui ont encore la force de vouloir, le désir de voyager ou de s'enrichir.

'Any where out of the world', on the other hand, finishes with an explosion of impotent and exasperated lyricism:

> Enfin, mon âme fait explosion, et sagement elle me crie: "N'importe où! n'importe où! pourvu que ce soit hors de ce monde!"

Here Baudelaire turns both his prose's inability to sustain lengthy poetic developments and his own lack of lyrical stamina to positive effect, the poem becoming, not the patiently elaborated unity so often achieved in *Les Fleurs du Mal*, but an initially wistful and finally explosive fragment.

No text in *Le Spleen de Paris* illustrates this type of prose poem better than 'L'Etranger', the first poem of the collection and, by common consent, a masterpiece of its kind. It reflects both the oblique, evasive nature of the later Baudelaire's expressed response to experience and yet the sudden, brief but explosive energy of his lyricism. Its evasiveness is manifested in the *étranger*'s refusal to give direct answers to questions and in the essentially cryptic nature of his one positive assertion which comes only at the very end of the poem. Its lyricism finds expression in similarly oblique and wistful phrases:

> —Ta patrie?
> —J'ignore sous quelle latitude elle est située.
> —La beauté?
> —Je l'aimerais volontiers, déesse et immortelle.

These, however, are transcended by the final explosive burst of poetic energy:

> —J'aime les nuages...les nuages qui passent...là-bas...là-bas...les merveilleux nuages!

Here, then, we have a text which is content merely to *announce* an immense area of poetic potential without actually realizing it: the text discovers a title, a vein, reaches the threshold of poetic experience but then breaks off, leaving, in a sense, the creation of the unrealized poem to the reader's imagination.

'Et à quoi bon exécuter des projets, puisque le projet est en lui-même une jouissance suffisante?', Baudelaire asks in 'Les Projets' and this attitude forms the aesthetic basis of more than one of his later prose poems. Thus 'Les Merveilleux Nuages' would be a marvellous title for a poem,[23] a poem which, in a sense, Baudelaire did not need to write, either because, as we have just seen, the project was in itself sufficient reward, or because that poem had already been written in his verse poetry. In 'Horreur sympathique' (1860) for example, written and published a year or so before 'L'Etranger', a specific interpretation is given to one aspect of the cloud image's enormous potential, the question and answer technique of this

---

[23] One which, a century later, was to prove irresistible even to a novelist, as is shown by Françoise Sagan's *Les Merveilleux Nuages*.

poem relating it even more closely to 'L'Etranger':

> De ce ciel bizarre et livide,
> Tourmenté comme ton destin,
> Quels pensers dans ton âme vide
> Descendent? réponds, libertin.

To which the *libertin* replies:

> Cieux déchirés comme de grèves,
> En vous se mire mon orgueil;
> Vos vastes nuages en deuil
> Sont les corbillards de mes rêves...

Similarly, in 'Any where out of the world', the final response of the provoked spirit comes like the announcement not merely of a different poem but also of a conception that could be realized only in *another* language.[24]

Another feature of many of Baudelaire's later prose poems which further emphasizes their enigmatic and fragmentary nature, is their essentially interrogative stance. Instead of comprehensively affirming the profound and mysterious significance of existence (as Baudelaire was so often to do in the idealizing poems of *Les Fleurs du Mal*) the texts of *Le Spleen de Paris* often take the shape of elaborate questions the indirect or cryptic answers to which seem to confirm a belief in the essential impenetrability of experience. We have noted how in 'L'Etranger' and 'Any where out of the world' answers to questions are essentially evasive or paradoxical. There are many other instances of this refusal to reassure doubt and satisfy curiosity. In 'Chacun sa chimère' we read:

> Je questionnai l'un de ces hommes, et je lui demandai où
> ils allaient ainsi. Il me répondit qu'il n'en savait rien, ni lui,
> ni les autres; mais qu'évidemment ils allaient

---

[24] The English source of the title 'Any where out of the world' is to be found in Thomas Hood's *The Bridge of Sighs* translated by Baudelaire in 1865. Here Baudelaire the *translator* discovers another fragment for exploitation by Baudelaire the *prose poet*.

quelque part, puisqu'ils étaient poussés par un invincible besoin de marcher

while in 'Le Fou et la Vénus', the *bouffon*'s pitiful plea is stonily ignored by the goddess:

Mais l'implacable Vénus regarde au loin je ne sais quoi avec ses yeux de marbre.

In 'Les Dons des fées', the questions posed by the shopkeeper, described as 'un de ces raisonneurs si communs, incapables de s'élever jusqu'à la logique de l'Absurde', whose son has quite unexpectedly received from the fairies the *gift of pleasing*, remain similarly unanswered by the exasperated fairy who retorts: ' "Parce que! parce que!" '. Turning her back, she comments to her colleagues on the vanity of the man who dares 'encore interroger et discuter l'indiscutable'. In 'Les Yeux des pauvres', thought, it is discovered, is essentially 'incommunicable', while in 'Mademoiselle Bistouri' an appeal for an explanation to the radical incomprehensibility of existence is desperately sought from the highest authority:

O Créateur! peut-il exister des monstres aux yeux de Celui-là seul qui sait pourquoi ils existent, comment ils *se sont faits* et comment ils auraient pu *ne pas se faire*?

It is an aspect of the peculiar modernity of the beings — human or supernatural — who inhabit the universe of *Le Spleen de Paris* that, when interrogated, *they do not know* or refuse to reply. They live in a world of radical uncertainty in which there are no longer positive truths — scientific, philosophical or religious — to supply the answers. *Le Spleen de Paris* is thus a world of strangers and outsiders, mystified beings whose existential incertitude is the sign of their modernity. The paths they seek out of their uncertainty are also disturbingly modern: their reactions are most commonly those of violence or indifference, with the occasional desperate recourse to prayer (as in 'A une heure du matin' and 'Mademoiselle Bistouri'). In

'Chacun sa chimère', for instance, we read:

> Et pendant quelques instants je m'obstinai à vouloir comprendre ce mystère; mais bientôt l'irrésistible Indifférence s'abattit sur moi...

and we remember in 'Le Port' the languorous pleasure of 'celui qui n'a plus ni curiosité ni ambition'. Rage and violence are, of course, the most common reactions to the impenetrability of experience, such explosions being expressed either in the modern image of shattering glass (as in 'Le Mauvais Vitrier' and 'La Femme sauvage et la petite-maîtresse' in which the poet threatens to throw his mistress out of the window 'comme une bouteille vide') or through other violent or sadistic gestures ('Une Mort héroïque', 'Portraits de maîtresses', 'Le Galant Tireur', 'Assommons les pauvres!').

This celebration of the irresponsible, almost gratuitous act is reflected in those sudden rhetorical questions (most often using formulae such as 'A quoi bon?', 'Qu'importe!', etc.) which bring many of the texts of *Le Spleen de Paris* to a close. In the last paragraph of 'Le Mauvais Vitrier', for example, such a formula expresses the perverse aestheticism of the irresponsible act: 'I did it for the *beauty* of it', the poet seems to be saying:

> Ces plaisanteries nerveuses ne sont pas sans péril, et on peut souvent les payer cher. Mais qu'importe l'éternité de la damnation à qui a trouvé dans une seconde l'infini de la jouissance?

The exasperated idealism of 'Les Fenêtres':

> Qu'importe ce que peut être la réalité placée hors de moi, si elle m'a aidé à vivre, à sentir que je suis et ce que je suis?

and the spiritual explosion already noted in 'Any where out of the world':

"N'importe où! n'importe où! Pourvu que ce soit hors de
ce monde!"

reflect similarly desperate and peremptory reactions to
experience.

What is original about Baudelaire's handling of the prose
poem in *Le Spleen de Paris* is that, in the later texts particularly,
he makes of the genre something radically different from what
had been achieved by predecessors such as Guérin and Bertrand
while at the same time creating something of a departure within
the context of his own work. With *Le Spleen de Paris* he was
beginning to move into territory previously uncharted either by
his predecessors or himself. The essentially *experimental* nature
of Baudelaire's prose poems is worth underlining here. Pichois
has described *Le Spleen de Paris* as a 'laboratoire d'expériences
dont les précipités diffèrent notablement' (I, 1301) and, as
Baudelaire himself admitted — not without irony — in his
preface to Houssaye (I, 267), his prose poems did not turn out
quite as expected. This could hardly have been otherwise, given
Baudelaire's fundamental commitment, in the prose poems, to
exploit the fugitive and accidental, to salvage fragments of
poetic perception as they surged from the humdrum of
experience or language. That he was not always successful in
discovering the right formula to express the moment's revelation
or that at times his experiments resulted in texts of only marginal
poetic value is undeniable. Nevertheless, it is sufficient that
Baudelaire does often reveal in a brief, disquieting or cryptic
fragment of text, those moments of poetic perception in which
'la profondeur de la vie se révèle tout entière dans le spectacle, si
ordinaire qu'il soit, qu'on a sous les yeux' (I, 659).

3. Le Spleen de Paris: *the texts*

(i) Problems of classification

Unlike those of *Les Fleurs du Mal*, in the consciously worked out architecture of which Baudelaire took considerable pride (see *30*, II, p.196), the texts which make up *Le Spleen de Paris* are not grouped under specific headings and do not, as a collection (which was not, of course, published as such until after his death), seem to follow a self-evident autobiographical or thematic plan. Baudelaire was quick to stress the apparently heterogeneous nature of his prose poems, describing them in his preface to Houssaye as a 'serpent' whose various 'tronçons' could be taken separately or together, enabling the reader to plot his own course through the 'tortueuse fantaisie' of the text and obviating any necessity, on the author's part, of channelling his fluid 'rêverie' into the 'fil interminable d'une intrigue superflue' (I, 275).

As with the problem of choosing the most appropriate title from various plausible alternatives, the discovery or imposition of a pattern underlying the apparently multifarious texts of *Le Spleen de Paris* is a critical problem the solution of which already seems to imply a certain interpretation of the work. Critics of *Le Spleen de Paris* have, for the most part, been aware of this. Accordingly, if they have cared to seek an overall framework at all, they have tended to seek a fairly loose one within which to place certain sub-groups of text (usually defined through related themes — see *5*, p.25) over which, though differing considerably, there has generally been less critical controversy. Pierre Moreau, for example, will take the *thyrse* motif, described by Baudelaire in the poem of that title, as a basic structural feature running through *Le Spleen de Paris* creating a spiral of *rêve/réalité* which, starting off in alternating texts — 'L'Etranger' (*rêve*), 'Le Désespoir de la vieille' (*réalité*)

— expands in gradually widening bands through the text as a whole (*23*, pp.44-47; see also, *17*, pp.144-53). The importance of the *thyrse* motif is also stressed by Georges Blin in one of the earliest (and best) studies of Baudelaire's prose poems, but Blin sees the only unifying feature of the texts in the collection as being their consistently *digressive* nature: 'tous les *Petits Poèmes en prose* ne présentent d'autre point commun que d'être écrits en *digression* délibérée' (*10*, p.166). Blin goes on to emphasize that this feature is as much a characteristic of the internal organization of isolated texts as of the collection as a whole: 'Telle est cette diversité qu'à l'intérieur d'une même pièce l'on assiste à de brusques changements de ton' (ibid).

The germ of a theory proposing the possibility of a unity concealed beneath the surface contradictions of *Le Spleen de Paris* is however to be found in the work of one of the earliest modern critics of Baudelaire's prose poems — that of Daniel-Rops who suggests:

> Tous ces éléments que nous venons de définir: sens de la misère humaine, goût impérieux du rêve, sentiment de captivité sur la terre, révolte contre ces liens, s'unissent et se sublimisent dans une donnée psychologique qu'on discerne, diffuse, tout le long des *Poèmes en prose*, bien qu'elle ne se manifeste pas très clairement (sauf dans deux poèmes, X, XLV): c'est le désespoir baudelairien, sentiment complexe où le dégoût du monde et l'espoir en Dieu, la cruauté et l'amour physique de la mort, se déchirent et s'accordent à la fois. Désespoir qui, au contraire de l'ennui romantique, ne cherche pas, trouvant le monde mauvais, à se louer soi-même dans la personnalité de l'auteur, mais veut au contraire signifier clairement que c'est dans cette personnalité même qu'il faut chercher la cause de tous les dégoûts et de toutes les faillites. C'est en ce point que s'achève la courbe générale des poèmes, et il est inutile de souligner combien était justifiée la prétention qu'avait Baudelaire d'avoir fait dans les *Petits Poèmes* une œuvre cohérente. (*13*, p.554)

Although Daniel-Rops does not insist dogmatically that *all* the texts of *Le Spleen de Paris* fit into this hypothetical structure, his theory is of particular interest in that, in suggesting the relevance of a psychoanalytical approach[25] to the Baudelairian prose poem, he anticipates by more than thirty years the application of this critical method to *Le Spleen de Paris* by Charles Mauron:

> Le poème des *Vocations*, par exemple, qui semble être en apparence un apologue poétique, paraît bien davantage, à qui l'analyse de près, une manière de confession peut-être inconsciente, qui eût offert précisément au freudisme l'occasion de justifier son utilité. (*13*, p.555)

In *Le Dernier Baudelaire*, the psychocritical method is used by Mauron to reveal the hidden coherence of what seems otherwise to be a work lacking unity. Mauron argues that certain basic *phantasmes*, interlinked in complex but coherent ways, provide the imaginative basis on which Baudelaire built the individual poems of *Le Spleen de Paris*. Though the latter can still be analyzed and evaluated in their own right by 'classical' criticism, they cannot be fully understood as a totality without close reference to Baudelaire's profound imaginative life. The 'chaînes d'identification' which structure the latter however, as Mauron takes pains to point out, do not constitute a reductive explanation but rather phenomena which themselves require explanation. Furthermore, in referring to Blin's study of Baudelaire's prose poems, mentioned above, Mauron does not see any contradiction between Blin's perception of the work's discontinuity and his own affirmation of its unity:

> les deux jugements ne me semblent pas contradictoires car ils résultent d'examens faits à des niveaux différents. La discontinuité appartient à l'elaboration de l'œuvre, la continuité à son noyau imaginatif profond. (*22*, p.129)

---

[25] The early attempt at a psychoanalysis of Baudelaire by René Laforgue in his *Echec de Baudelaire, étude psychanalytique sur la névrose de Charles Baudelaire* (Paris: Denoël et Steele, 1931), Daniel-Rops dismisses as 'médiocre'.

Fascinating and coherent though Mauron's schema is, being more concerned with the 'serpent entier' than with the separate 'tronçons', it does not always help the reader in his attempt to adopt an approach to the individual texts as, weaving his way systematically or haphazardly through the volume, he happens upon them. What is proposed in the next few pages therefore is a system of classification which, within a framework provided by the work's fundamental 'morality'/'lyricism' polarity (and polarity, here, must not be seen as implying simple opposition), will enable individual texts to be placed in plausible formal categories which, while reflecting the shifting tensions and emphases within the work, will also reflect its overall balance and unity.

Turning to Figure I then, we see that, as one might expect, Baudelaire's lyricism finds expression in texts which can, fairly loosely, be described as *poems* whereas Baudelaire *moraliste* was a writer of *essais* and *contes*, and that these basic categories, representing the two extremes — 'poetic' and 'prosaic' — of literary expression in *Le Spleen de Paris*, numerically balance each other out. It was suggested, in Chapter 2, that it was a characteristic of *Le Spleen de Paris* that the moralist in Baudelaire appeared to be beginning to oust the poet. If however this does not seem to be reflected in the diagram, this is because, as we saw, Baudelaire started as a *poet* in prose (with 'Le Crépuscule du soir', 'La Solitude', 'Les Projets', 'L'Horloge', 'Un Hémisphère dans une chevelure' and 'L'Invitation au voyage', all of which are to be found in the *poème* column) and shifted his interest from poetic evocation to concern with moral analysis only gradually as *Le Spleen de Paris* began to take shape.

But what are the criteria applied here in placing the texts of *Le Spleen de Paris* in the various categories and what is the rationale behind the latter? In many ways those categories which embrace the largest number of texts are easiest to justify. *Poems* are those texts, usually quite short, which, fundamentally lyrical in style, structure themselves round or lead up to some vivid or explosive image.[26] At the opposite end of the scale, the

[26] It is interesting, by way of corroboration, that in selecting Baudelairian texts for his *Anthologie du poème en prose*, Chapelan did not choose any text from *Le*

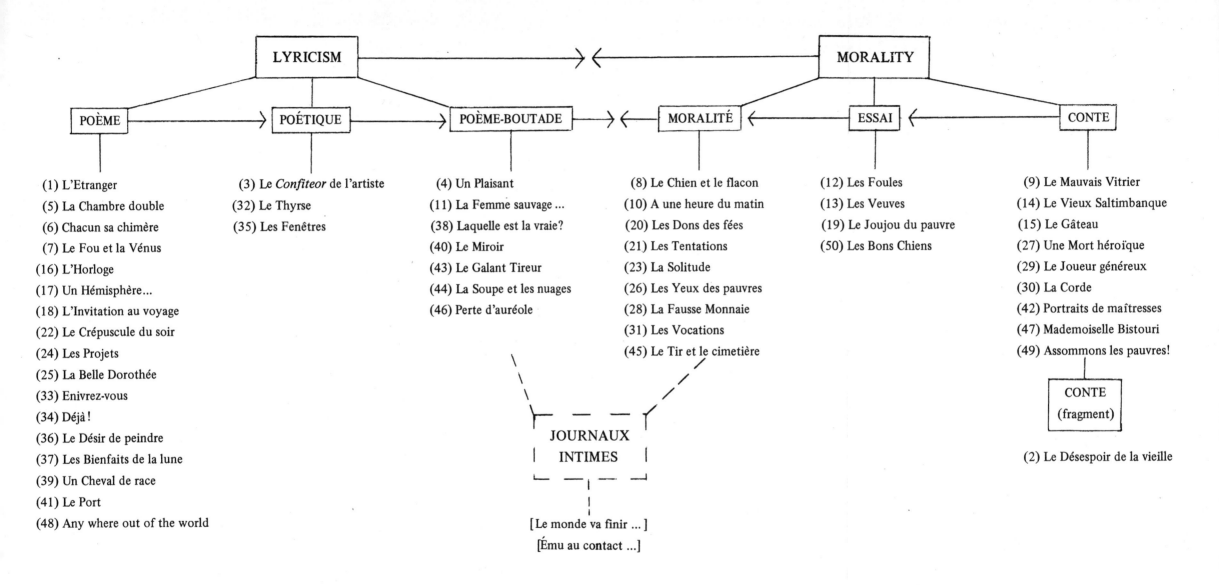

Fig. I: TOWARDS A FORMAL CLASSIFICATION OF 'LE SPLEEN DE PARIS'

conventional literary genres such as *conte* and *essai* are relatively easily identified by their essentially narrative or discursive style, the distinction between the two genres being based on the plot or story interest which, almost by definition, must be seen to be stronger in the former category. Indeed, most Baudelairian texts in the *conte* category share that sober austerity of style, narrative economy and often cruel irony of tone, associated with certain nineteenth-century storytellers — whether Edgar Allan Poe, whose influence on Baudelaire the storyteller was decisive, or Maupassant whose cynical pessimism is remarkably anticipated in such *contes* or fragments of *conte* as 'La Corde' and 'Le Désespoir de la vieille'. The *essais*, on the other hand, are characterized by an essentially digressive style, the consistent use of the plural in their titles — 'Les Foules', 'Les Veuves', 'Les Bons Chiens' — being itself sufficiently indicative of the fact that the principal interest of these texts will lie as much in the exploration of a particular *subject* as in the relating of a story. Furthermore, certain texts, such as 'Le Joujou du pauvre', are known to derive from a longer essay of an earlier date.

However, it is hoped that Figure I will go further, in focussing attention on the much more problematic categories of the Baudelairian prose poem (in relation to other texts both within and without the collection): those, that is, which fall outside the more clear-cut generical distinctions between *poème*, *essai* and *conte*. Of these three—*poétique*, *poème-boutade* and *moralité*—the *moralité* category (like its neighbours under the general heading *Morality*) is perhaps the least difficult to justify, especially if varying meanings of the word *moralité* are allowed. If, as suggested by Pichois (I, 1300), the word is taken in its medieval sense of Morality (-play), the moral phantasmagoria such as 'Les Dons des fées', 'Les Tentations' and, to a lesser extent, 'Les Vocations', naturally fall into this group.[27] If, in

Spleen de Paris that is not to be found under the general heading of *lyricism* in the present classification, all but two of Chapelan's titles from the prose poems in fact appearing in the *poème* category. The two exceptions — 'Le *Confiteor* de l'artiste' and 'La Soupe et les nuages' — appear here respectively in the two related groups of *poétique* and *poème-boutade*.

[27] For André Breton, in his *Manifeste du surréalisme* (1924) (Coll. Idées, Paris: Gallimard, 1969, p.39), Baudelaire was 'surréaliste dans la morale'; this formula expresses well the bizarre or oneiric quality of the moral parables in the *moralité* category.

addition, the word *moralité* is taken as meaning a more general demonstration of moral lesson or intent, then 'La Solitude' (with its references to the maxims of La Bruyère and Pascal), the epigrammatic 'Le Chien et le flacon', the confession-like 'A une heure du matin' and 'La Fausse Monnaie' and 'Le Tir et le cimetière', with their more or less explicit moral reflections, can also be included in this group.

The small group of texts listed under the heading *poétique* need not delay us long since, in a way, it is merely an outgrowth of the more general category of *poème*. This group is, nevertheless, significant since the three poems in it — 'Le *Confiteor* de l'artiste', 'Le Thyrse', 'Les Fenêtres' — having as their essential theme the operations of the creative psyche, contrive, as well as being themselves poems, to establish a theoretical basis for a poetic method, or *poétique*, that is of more general relevance to *Le Spleen de Paris* as a whole. The dual ambition of these texts, one simultaneously poetic and theoretical, is reflected in the tension between lyricism and philosophizing or moralizing, that is, between poetic evocation and moral or analytical self-examination, which, as has already been noted, was a more general characteristic of Baudelaire's prose poems. Thus, 'Le Thyrse' and 'Les Fenêtres', starting as calm and philosophical enquiries, end with a burst of lyricism while 'Le *Confiteor* de l'artiste' reverses the process, starting with a lyrical flourish and ending with a philosophical *pointe*.

A characteristic which the *poétique* category of prose poem shares with those of *moralité* and *poème-boutade* is a close relationship with many of the fragments which make up the *Journaux intimes*. In a sense, *Fusées* and, to a lesser extent, the more consciously planned *Mon Cœur mis à nu*, represent a kind of workshop of Baudelairian ideas, attitudes and themes, amongst which fragments of poem, moral epigram or aesthetic theory are stored before being refined and re-directed towards other parts of Baudelaire's *œuvre* as finished works in their own right. The plan of 'Le Galant Tireur', for example, is to be found in *Fusées* XI (I, 660) and the existence of such prototypes has led commentators and anthologizers of Baudelaire the prose poet to cite as potential prose poems texts from the *Journaux intimes* which were not in fact to appear in *Le Spleen de Paris*. Thus, Chapelan includes in his *Anthologie du poème en prose* that remarkable fragmênt from *Fusées* which begins 'Le monde va finir' (I, 655) while Pierre Jean Jouve, in an article on *Le Spleen de Paris* (*20*, pp. 32-39), suggests the inclusion of another passage from the same section of *Fusées* — that beginning: 'Emu au contact de ces voluptés' (I, 664).

Of all the categories of Baudelairian prose poem so far suggested, none is more closely related to the *Journaux intimes* than that of the *poème-boutade* for which Baudelaire's statement from *Fusées* (I, 668): 'J'ai cultivé mon hystérie avec jouissance et terreur',[28] would form a fitting epigraph. The term *poème-boutade* has been suggested by Henri Lemaitre to describe

> une sorte de genre littéraire auquel il semble, d'après certains passages des *Journaux intimes*, que Baudelaire ait aimé s'exercer...où tout un monde de désillusions et de rancœurs se ramasse dans une incisive brièveté. (*4*, p.185)

This category of poem naturally finds itself near the frontiers between lyricism and morality, because it is in these borderline regions that the tension between the two poles is most acutely felt. Sharing (with the exception of the rather longer 'La Femme sauvage et la petite-maîtresse') the incisive brevity of the moral epigram but also the often explosive energy of the lyrical fragment, these curiously schizophrenic texts give expression to a series of paradoxes and confrontations in which perversity finds an outlet in sadism or violence and fatuousness in black humour. It is in these texts that Baudelaire the realist and Baudelaire the poet clash, the realist in 'La Soupe et les nuages' parodying the poet of 'L'Etranger', the artist hero of 'Le *Confiteor*' being reduced to fatuousness in 'Perte d'auréole' while the *galant* of 'Un Hémisphère dans une chevelure' and 'L'Invitation au voyage' shows himself in quite different colours

[28] See also Baudelaire's remark, in a letter to his mother of March 1865, which, though referring to *Le Spleen de Paris* as a whole, may be seen to apply in particular to those texts in the *poème-boutade* category: 'J'associerai l'effrayant avec le bouffon, et même la tendresse avec la haine' (II, 473).

in 'La Femme sauvage et la petite-maîtresse' and 'Le Galant Tireur'. Poet and realist, it may be objected, also exchange blows, sometimes fatal ones, in texts outside the *poème-boutade* category such as 'Le Mauvais Vitrier', 'Une Mort héroïque' and 'Assommons les pauvres!'. But in these three instances, the violent or sadistic tendency is translated into a protracted action necessitating a narrative development which is structured by the form of the *conte*. In texts in the *poème-boutade* category, however — and this is one of the reasons why they are *boutades* — the violence or sadism (with the one exception of the (playful?) thump in the back of 'La Soupe et les nuages') is only threatened (as in 'La Femme sauvage et la petite-maîtresse'), indirect ('Le Galant Tireur') or imaginary (as in 'Laquelle est la vraie?'), a factor which contributes to the bizarre tonality of the texts in this group.

The chief aim of the above notes has been to establish a pattern of classification which, it is hoped, will be taken as much as a basis for argument and discussion as a fixed and immutable system. It is for this reason, partly, that two of its governing principles have been those of flexibility and eclecticism. The system's flexibility lies in its tolerance of a certain amount of overlapping of items without the overall structure collapsing, while its eclecticism is reflected in the attempt to bring together and coordinate various useful but isolated suggestions towards a classification the sources of which are to be found not only in *Le Spleen de Paris*'s various editors and commentators, but also in some suggestions made by Baudelaire himself.[29]

(ii) *The prose poet as 'promeneur solitaire': settings and contexts in 'Le Spleen de Paris'*

The history of prose poetry in France has been virtually synonymous with that of the Romantic *promeneur solitaire*.

[29] Among the lists of 'poëmes à faire' (see *2*, pp.155-60), which Baudelaire drew up for *Le Spleen de Paris* in the 1860s, are to be found the headings: *rêves*, or *oneirocrities*, *symboles et moralités* and *choses parisiennes* (with, on occasion, the additional note: *Autres classes à trouver*), which are not without bearing on the system proposed here. The *symboles et moralités* heading, for example, might happily embrace the problematic categories of *poétique*, *poème-boutade* and *moralité*.

Rousseau was the great originator of the tradition with *Les Rêveries du promeneur solitaire* which was both a 'recueil...de longs rêves'[30] and an attempt by the individual during lonely wanderings to feel and understand the true nature of his existence. This double quest — for it was emotional as well as philosophical — was naturally to seek expression in a language capable of both lyricism and analysis, one that was able at the same time to record an instinctive, spontaneous response to phenomena and to *situate* that response in a broader rational or social perspective. Rousseau, being both philosopher and imaginative writer, was well suited to discovering a language of this sort; an essential part of the charm and the originality of the *Rêveries* lies in the fact that they allow the writer's childlike naivety and the philosopher's deep intelligence an even share of fulfilment.

A similar tension between philosophy and *rêverie* is fundamental to *Le Spleen de Paris* and reflects the radical contradictions inherent in the stance of *promeneur solitaire*, a vocation which, as Baudelaire implies in 'Les Veuves', is that both of 'poète' and 'philosophe'. In becoming a *promeneur* of the city, the philosopher side of the Baudelairian personality tries to lure the poet out of his seclusion and into the street, to force him to confront reality in all its recalcitrance and incomprehensibility while, at the same time, the poet alone is able to provide the *philosophe* with a viable alternative if reality should, as often happened, prove intractable to philosophy's systems. The theoretical basis of the *philosophe*'s standpoint is sketched at the beginning of 'La Corde', in which Baudelaire writes:

Les illusions...sont aussi innombrables peut-être que les rapports des hommes entre eux, ou des hommes avec les choses. Et quand l'illusion disparaît, c'est-à-dire quand nous voyons l'être ou le fait tel qu'il existe en dehors de nous, nous éprouvons un bizarre sentiment, compliqué moitié de regret pour le fantôme disparu, moitié de surprise agréable devant la nouveauté, devant le fait réel.

[30] *Les Rêveries du promeneur solitaire*, ed. J. Voisine, p.123.

The point of view of the artist is established in 'Le *Confiteor* de l'artiste':

> Grand délice que celui de noyer son regard dans l'immensité du ciel et de la mer! Solitude, silence, incomparable chasteté de l'azur! une petite voile frissonnante à l'horizon, et qui par sa petitesse et son isolement imite mon irrémédiable existence, mélodie monotone de la houle, toutes ces choses pensent par moi, ou je pense par elles (car dans la grandeur de la rêverie, le *moi* se perd vite!); elles pensent, dis-je, mais musicalement et pittoresquement, sans arguties, sans syllogismes, sans déductions.

In 'Assommons les pauvres!' we see the victory of the philosopher:

> — ô miracle! ô jouissance du philosophe qui vérifie l'excellence de sa théorie!

while in 'Mademoiselle Bistouri', philosophy's failure to explain the 'bizarreries' encountered 'dans une grande ville, quand on sait se promener et regarder' is reflected in the poet's desperate appeal to 'Celui-là seul qui sait pourquoi ils existent, comment ils *se sont faits* et comment ils auraient pu *ne pas se faire*'.

The alternating victories of poet and philosopher (but also the occasional stalemate such as that noted in 'Mademoiselle Bistouri') are naturally reflected not only in the forms but also in the settings and contexts in *Le Spleen de Paris*. Thus, as Figure II tries to show, those texts in which the setting is the street or the suburb, the public park or roadway, most often reflect a concern with the verification of the reality of the outside world ('l'être ou le fait tel qu'il existe en dehors de nous'). This reality finds expression in the more prosaic genres of *conte*, *essai* and *moralité*, those, that is, which seem best suited to expressing the moral or philosophical conclusions drawn from the *promeneur*'s 'accidents de la flânerie'.[31] This does not mean, of

[31] An important exception to this general tendency is a sub-group of

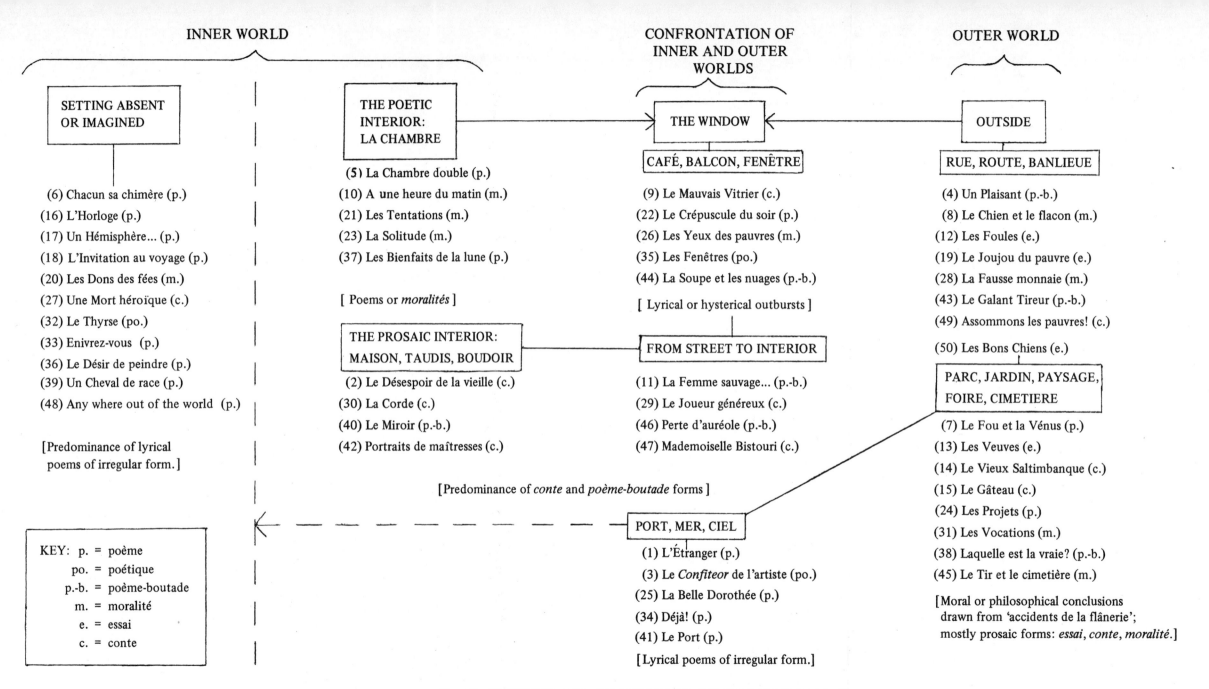

INNER WORLD

CONFRONTATION OF INNER AND OUTER WORLDS

OUTER WORLD

SETTING ABSENT OR IMAGINED

(6) Chacun sa chimère (p.)
(16) L'Horloge (p.)
(17) Un Hémisphère... (p.)
(18) L'Invitation au voyage (p.)
(20) Les Dons des fées (m.)
(27) Une Mort héroïque (c.)
(32) Le Thyrse (po.)
(33) Enivrez-vous (p.)
(36) Le Désir de peindre (p.)
(39) Un Cheval de race (p.)
(48) Any where out of the world (p.)

[Predominance of lyrical poems of irregular form.]

KEY: p. = poème
po. = poétique
p.-b. = poème-boutade
m. = moralité
e. = essai
c. = conte

THE POETIC INTERIOR: LA CHAMBRE

(5) La Chambre double (p.)
(10) A une heure du matin (m.)
(21) Les Tentations (m.)
(23) La Solitude (m.)
(37) Les Bienfaits de la lune (p.)

[Poems or *moralités*]

THE PROSAIC INTERIOR: MAISON, TAUDIS, BOUDOIR

(2) Le Désespoir de la vieille (c.)
(30) La Corde (c.)
(40) Le Miroir (p.-b.)
(42) Portraits de maîtresses (c.)

[Predominance of *conte* and *poème-boutade* forms]

THE WINDOW

CAFÉ, BALCON, FENÊTRE

(9) Le Mauvais Vitrier (c.)
(22) Le Crépuscule du soir (p.)
(26) Les Yeux des pauvres (m.)
(35) Les Fenêtres (po.)
(44) La Soupe et les nuages (p.-b.)

[Lyrical or hysterical outbursts]

FROM STREET TO INTERIOR

(11) La Femme sauvage... (p.-b.)
(29) Le Joueur généreux (c.)
(46) Perte d'auréole (p.-b.)
(47) Mademoiselle Bistouri (c.)

PORT, MER, CIEL

(1) L'Étranger (p.)
(3) Le *Confiteor* de l'artiste (po.)
(25) La Belle Dorothée (p.)
(34) Déjà! (p.)
(41) Le Port (p.)

[Lyrical poems of irregular form.]

OUTSIDE

RUE, ROUTE, BANLIEUE

(4) Un Plaisant (p.-b.)
(8) Le Chien et le flacon (m.)
(12) Les Foules (e.)
(19) Le Joujou du pauvre (e.)
(28) La Fausse monnaie (m.)
(43) Le Galant Tireur (p.-b.)
(49) Assommons les pauvres! (c.)
(50) Les Bons Chiens (e.)

PARC, JARDIN, PAYSAGE, FOIRE, CIMETIERE

(7) Le Fou et la Vénus (p.)
(13) Les Veuves (e.)
(14) Le Vieux Saltimbanque (c.)
(15) Le Gâteau (c.)
(24) Les Projets (p.)
(31) Les Vocations (m.)
(38) Laquelle est la vraie? (p.-b.)
(45) Le Tir et le cimetière (m.)

[Moral or philosophical conclusions drawn from 'accidents de la flânerie'; mostly prosaic forms: *essai, conte, moralité*.]

Fig. II: SETTINGS AND CONTEXTS OF 'LE SPLEEN DE PARIS'

course, that those texts in which settings and contexts are essentially *interior*, as opposed to exterior, by that token alone reflect an inner, more imaginative or poetic world. For as Figure II again tries to show, various important intermediary stages complicate the symmetry of the inner/outer world polarity.

In the first place, in one group of prose poems, a significant shift of context or setting takes place *within* individual texts. Thus in 'Le Joueur généreux', 'Perte d'auréole' and 'Mademoiselle Bistouri', there is a movement from street to interior; but this shift of perspective reflects a move from a real and recognizable world into a bizarre ('Mademoiselle Bistouri'), imaginary ('Perte d'auréole') or supernatural ('Le Joueur généreux') domain. 'La Femme sauvage et la petite-maîtresse', the fourth poem in this group, poses particular problems, since the context of this *poème-conversation* seems constantly to shift from inside to outside and back again; the original setting appears to be interior: with the description of the *femme sauvage*, however, we are already outside in the fairground, but seem to have returned inside by the end of the text, since the poem ends with the poet's threat of throwing his mistress out of the window (although it is possible that the whole conversation, threats included, was carried on at the fairground).

The window, of course, is both the *image* and the *context* of confrontations between poet and philosopher, between inner and outer worlds.[32] At the end of 'La femme sauvage...' we see the poet asserting his right to behave as a punitive moralist:

"Tant poète que je sois, je ne suis pas aussi dupe que vous voudriez le croire, et si vous me fatiguez trop souvent de

poems (listed under the heading *Port, mer, ciel* in Figure II) in which the poet's gaze is directed skywards or seawards. Since the lyrical fragments which make up this group have more in common with those essentially poetic texts the setting of which is absent or imagined, discussion of them will be deferred until later in this section.

[32] See Graham Chesters, 'The Transformation of a prose poem: Baudelaire's"Crépuscule du soir" ' in *Baudelaire, Mallarmé, Valéry: new essays in honour of Lloyd James Austin* (ed. M. Bowie, A. Fairlie, A. Finch, Cambridge: University Press, 1982), p.27.

> vos *précieuses* pleurnicheries, je vous traiterai en *femme
> sauvage*, ou je vous jetterai par la fenêtre, comme une
> bouteille vide''

and the threat of defenestration is, in effect, a threat of
exclusion from the ideal world experienced behind or perceived
through the glass of the window.[33] In 'Les Fenêtres',[34]
Baudelaire develops the implications of his poetic philosophy of
the window:

> Celui qui regarde du dehors à travers une fenêtre
> ouverte, ne voit jamais autant de choses que celui qui
> regarde une fenêtre fermée. Il n'est pas d'objet plus
> profond, plus mystérieux, plus fécond, plus ténébreux,
> plus éblouissant qu'une fenêtre éclairée d'une chandelle.
> Ce qu'on peut voir au soleil est toujours moins intéressant
> que ce qui se passe derrière une vitre. Dans ce trou noir ou
> lumineux vit la vie, rêve la vie, souffre la vie.

This poem ends with one of the most positive vindications of the
rights of the poet (as opposed to those of the philosopher) in all
Baudelaire's prose poems:

> Qu'importe ce que peut être la réalité placée hors de moi, si
> elle m'a aidé à vivre, à sentir que je suis et ce que je suis?

The *Café/balcon/fenêtre* group of poems in Figure II all
express this confrontation between inner and outer worlds from
settings — café terrace, balcony and window — which mark the
frontier between a mysterious interior world and the banality of
the street or, alternatively, an infinite vista of sky and the
drabness of a banal interior. In 'Les Fenêtres', as we have seen,
and in 'Le Crépuscule du soir', the poet's idealizing gaze is able

---

[33] One might say that the mistress is discarded as a *bouteille vide* because, like
an empty glass container, she is devoid of that *spirit* so ardently sought by the
poet.

[34] See Sima Naomi Godfrey's interesting commentary on this poem in her
unpublished thesis 'Fenêtres sur la vie moderne: the *Petits Poèmes en prose* and a
Baudelairian Motif' (Cornell University, 1978), pp.25-74.

to harmonize and interpret the disparate sensations aroused by the scene before him, creating of them either a *legend*, as in 'Les Fenêtres':

> Par-delà des vagues de toits, j'aperçois une femme...j'ai refait l'histoire de cette femme, ou plutôt sa légende

or some other imaginative *fantaisie*, as in 'Le Crépuscule du soir':

> le soir, en fumant et en contemplant le repos de l'immense vallée, hérissée de maisons dont chaque fenêtre dit: "C'est ici la paix maintenant; c'est ici la joie de la famille!" je puis, quand le vent souffle de là-haut, bercer ma pensée étonnée à cette imitation des harmonies de l'enfer.
>
> ...
>
> et les étoiles vacillantes d'or et d'argent...représentent ces feux de la fantaisie qui ne s'allument bien que sous le deuil profond de la Nuit.

In 'Le Mauvais Vitrier', 'Les Yeux des pauvres' and 'La Soupe et les nuages', however, it is the philosopher who, with some (often literally) shattering gesture, breaks the glass of illusion protecting the inner from the outer world. In 'Le Mauvais Vitrier', for example, the 'pot de fleurs' (which in 'Un Hémisphère dans une chevelure' had decorated the poetic 'chambre d'un beau navire') is dropped from the balcony on to the glass-seller, causing the latter to fall and smash his load of panes to the hysterical delight of the philosopher/poet. In 'La Soupe et les nuages', the realist/philosopher takes the form of the poet's mistress who gets her revenge on the fantasizing poet with a thump in the back and the following outburst:

> "— Allez-vous bientôt manger votre soupe, s... b... de marchand de nuages?"

Meanwhile, in 'Les Yeux des pauvres', the poet's hopes of a perfect union of his own with his mistress's soul are hopelessly shattered when her reaction to the eyes of the poor, who are gazing at them on the café terrace, is seen to be radically at odds with his own, leading him to draw the essentially *philosophical* conclusion that 'la pensée est incommunicable, même entre gens qui s'aiment!'

'Ainsi, quand le promeneur des *Petits Poèmes en prose* rentre dans sa chambre, il rêve...' affirms Mauron (*22*, p.70) and, in effect, the vast majority of the texts which reflect the inner world of the poet either specify or imply an interior setting as the *point de départ* of their reveries. The intention of those poems in which a setting of *chambre* is given (and the *chambre* setting must not be confused with the altogether more *public* interiors of *maison* or *boudoir d'hommes*, etc., which provide the décor for a distinct and much more prosaic group of texts), is basically that of establishing a scenario against which some spiritual action or development — poetic or moral — can take place. Thus, in 'Les Bienfaits de la lune', the moon descends a staircase of clouds to pass silently through the window into the room to perform its bizarre rites, while in 'Les Tentations', the 'Deux superbes Satans' and the 'Diablesse' enter by an imaginary staircase to perform their *moralité* before the sleeping poet. In 'A une heure du matin', the poet has sought the privacy of his chamber to devote himself to a moral self-examination in which the essentially religious rites of confession and prayer contrast with the altogether more philosophical approach to the question of solitude adumbrated in the poem of that title; for in 'La Solitude', it is the philosopher rather than the poet who discourses calmly and urbanely on the merits of seclusion, citing Pascal and La Bruyère in support of his argument.

Like the poetic state for which it will often provide the context or the inspiration ('Une chambre qui ressemble à une rêverie, une chambre véritablement *spirituelle*, où l'atmosphère stagnante est légèrement teintée de rose et de bleu'), the poet's privacy and solitude is a fragile and precarious phenomenon, excessively vulnerable to disturbance or intrusion from without:

D'abord, un double tour à la serrure. Il me semble que ce tour de clef augmentera ma solitude et fortifiera les barricades qui me séparent actuellement du monde.

Baudelaire reminds himself here, in 'A une heure du matin', that failure to take such precautions can have disastrous results. This is demonstrated in 'La Chambre double' in which the spectre which enters the room is not from some spiritual or supernatural domain but from the real world; its presence is sufficient to shatter the illusions so poetically constructed in the first half of the poem (the opening section of which was cited above):

> Horreur! je me souviens! je me souviens! Oui! ce taudis, ce séjour de l'éternel ennui, est bien le mien. Voici les meubles sots, poudreux, écornés; la cheminée sans flamme et sans braise, souillée de crachats; les tristes fenêtres où la pluie a tracé des sillons dans la poussière; les manuscrits, raturés ou incomplets; l'almanach où le crayon a marqué les dates sinistres!

With such shifts from fantasy to reality, there is a movement from the ideal world of poetry to that of the nineteenth-century realist novel or short story, a world in which a prosaic interior provided the setting for a very different kind of action from that of the sensuous or suggestive lyric. Thus the *Maison, taudis, boudoir* group of texts (in which the range of interior décor, like its typical forms (*conte* or *poème-boutade*), is shared with the adjacent group of texts — that which includes 'Perte d'auréole' and 'Madamoiselle Bistouri') exemplify a world Maupassant was later to make entirely his own, a world of banal interiors in which, nevertheless, the bizarre happened, the grotesque existed and the unspeakable was blandly recounted.

Just as the world of the prosaic interior has much in common with that of the Parisian street or suburb, so, paradoxically, those texts in which the point of departure is the contemplation of some vast vista of the natural world (almost invariably sea or sky) are closely related to those poems of an essentially inner world in which the setting is unspecified or imaginary. In some instances, indeed (particularly those involving exoticism: 'Un Hémisphère dans une chevelure', 'L'Invitation au voyage'; 'La

Belle Dorothée'), it is arguable whether settings are in fact real or imagined. But this does not really matter since the essential function of the lyrical fragments which predominate in both groups is to express that fleeting glimpse of the infinite or absolute which, as was seen in Chapter 2, was to be the achievement of Baudelaire's most original and successful prose poems.

If some time has been spent exploring the shifts and fluctuations in attitude and style of the prose poems of *Le Spleen de Paris*, it is because they so vividly reflect the loss of spiritual bearings of the modern consciousness they express. Although the philosophical and moral element in the Baudelairian personality is asserted, sometimes aggressively, throughout *Le Spleen de Paris*, giving rise to the splenetic tone which pervades the collection, there does not always seem to be, on Baudelaire's part, profound commitment to the lessons he administers: there is even about his most forceful gestures ('Le Mauvais Vitrier', 'Assommons les pauvres!') more than a smack of the *boutade*. But, more seriously in a writer whose fundamental vocation is, after all, that of poetry, the poet too (as was seen in the last chapter) seems to be experiencing a crisis of confidence. Poetic insights are snatched desperately from brief interludes in the frustration or boredom that the pace and style of modern urban life impose upon him but are no longer susceptible of extended development: a glimpse of passing clouds between conversations may provide the authentic poetic *frisson* but does not, as say, the sonnet 'Correspondances' did, provide the basis of a coherent and imaginatively satisfying conception of the universe. As Jean Starobinski has shown (*28*, pp.88-92), 'Une Mort héroïque' was but one of the first in a series of later nineteenth-century parables illustrating the truth that the artist never pirouettes so superbly as when he does so over the void. *Le Spleen de Paris*'s elaborate rehearsals of moral and philosophical stances thus may be no more than performances and Art only the ultimate *boutade*. But the profound morality and philosophy of Baudelaire lie in his absolute commitment, in spite of his doubts, to the aesthetic moment:

> qu'importe l'éternité de la damnation à qui a trouvé dans
> une seconde l'infini de la jouissance?

he asks in 'Le Mauvais Vitrier', as we saw, and in 'Les Fenêtres':

> Qu'importe ce que peut être la réalité placée hors de moi, si
> elle m'a aidé à vivre, à sentir que je suis et ce que je suis?

No modern writer made such heroic and radical gestures stand
out more beautifully and authentically from banal or prosaic
contexts than did the Baudelaire of *Le Spleen de Paris*.

Select Bibliography

I EDITIONS OF LE SPLEEN DE PARIS

1   Daniel-Rops, *Petits Poèmes en prose (Le Spleen de Paris)*, Paris: Les Belles-Lettres, 1934

2   Kopp, Robert, *Petits Poëmes en prose*, Paris: Corti, 1969

3   ——, *Petits Poëmes en prose*, Paris: Gallimard, Coll. Poésie, 1973

4   Lemaitre, Henri, *Petits Poèmes en prose (Le Spleen de Paris)*, Paris: Garnier, 1962

5   Milner, Max, *Le Spleen de Paris. Petits poèmes en prose*, Paris: Imprimerie Nationale, Coll. Lettres françaises, 1979

6   Pichois, Claude, *Le Spleen de Paris* in *Œuvres complètes*, I, Paris: Gallimard, Bibliothèque de la Pléiade, 1975 (see *29* below)

7   Roy, Claude, *Le Spleen de Paris* (texte de 1869), Paris: Livre de Poche, 1964

8   Ruff, Marcel, *Petits Poèmes en prose (Le Spleen de Paris)*, Paris: Garnier-Flammarion, 1967

9   Zimmermann, Melvin, *Petits Poèmes en prose*, Manchester: University Press, 1968

II STUDIES RELATING (WHOLLY OR IN PART) TO LE SPLEEN DE PARIS

10   Blin, Georges, 'Introduction aux *Petits Poèmes en prose*', in *Le Sadisme de Baudelaire*, Paris: Corti, 1948, pp.141-77

11   ——, 'Les Fleurs de l'impossible', *Revue des Sciences Humaines*, XXXII (1967), pp.461-66

12   Bornecque, Jacques-Henri, 'Les Poèmes en prose de Baudelaire', *L'Information Littéraire*, V (1953), pp.177-82

13   Daniel-Rops, 'Baudelaire, poète en prose', *La Grande Revue*, XXXV (1931), pp.534-55

14   Fairlie, Alison, 'Observations sur les *Petits Poèmes en prose*', *Revue des Sciences Humaines*, XXXII (1967), pp.449-60

15   ——, 'Quelques remarques sur les *Petits Poèmes en prose*', in *Baudelaire: Actes du colloque de Nice (1967): Annales de la Facultés des*

Lettres et des Sciences Humaines de Nice, 1968, Paris: Les Belles-Lettres, 1968, pp.89-97

16   Galand, René, *Baudelaire: poétiques et poésie*, Paris: Nizet, 1969, pp.461-525

17   George, F.M.de, 'The Structure of Baudelaire's *Petits Poèmes en prose*', *L'Esprit Créateur*, XIII (1973), pp.144-53

18   Johnson, Barbara, *Défigurations du langage poétique: la seconde révolution baudelairienne*, Paris: Flammarion, 1979

19   ——, 'Quelques conséquences de la différence anatomique des textes. Pour une théorie du poème en prose', *Poétique*, 28 (1976), pp.450-65

20   Jouve, Pierre Jean, '*Le Spleen de Paris*', *Mercure de France*, CCCXXII (1951), pp.32-39

21   Leblois, André, *Prestige et actualité des 'Petits Poèmes en prose' de Baudelaire*, Paris: Minard, Archives des Lettres Modernes, XVIII, 1958

22   Mauron, Charles, *Le Dernier Baudelaire*, Paris: Corti, 1966

23   Moreau, Pierre, *La Tradition française du poème en prose avant Baudelaire*, Paris: Minard, Archives des Lettres Modernes, XIX-XX, 1959

24   ——, 'En marge du *Spleen de Paris*', *Revue d'Histoire Littéraire de la France*, LIX (1959), pp.539-43

25   Peyre, Henri, *Connaissance de Baudelaire*, Paris: Corti, 1951, pp. 134-40

26   Porché, François, *Baudelaire, histoire d'une âme*, Paris: Flammarion, 1944, pp.390-95

27   Ruff, Marcel, *Baudelaire*, Paris: Hatier, Connaissance des Lettres, 1957, pp.170-80

28   Starobinski, Jean, *Portrait de l'artiste en saltimbanque*, Geneva: Skira, Les Sentiers de la création, 1970, pp.88-92

III GENERAL WORKS RELATING TO BAUDELAIRE OR TO THE PROSE POEM

29   Baudelaire, Charles, *Œuvres complètes*, ed. Claude Pichois, 2 vols, Paris: Gallimard, Bibliothèque de la Pléiade, 1975-76

30   ——, *Correspondance*, ed. Cl. Pichois & J. Ziegler, 2 vols, Paris: Gallimard, Bibliothèque de la Pléiade, 1973

31   Benjamin, Walter, *Charles Baudelaire: a lyric poet in the era of high capitalism* (trans. H. Zohn), London: NLB, 1973

32   Bernard, Suzanne, *Le Poème en prose de Baudelaire jusqu'à nos jours*,
        Paris: Nizet, 1959

33   Chapelan, Maurice, *Anthologie du poème en prose*, Paris: Julliard
        Sequana, 1946

34   Chérel, Albert, *La Prose poétique française*, Paris: L'Artisan du livre,
        1940

35   Citron, Pierre, 'La Poésie du Paris de Baudelaire', in *La Poésie de Paris
        dans la littérature française de Rousseau à Baudelaire*, 2 vols, Paris:
        Editions de Minuit, 1961, pp.332-83

36   Scott, Clive, 'The Prose Poem and Free Verse', in *Modernism*, ed. M.
        Bradbury & J. McFarlane, Harmondsworth: Penguin, Pelican Guides to
        European Literature, 1976, pp.349-68

CRITICAL GUIDES TO FRENCH TEXTS

edited by
Roger Little, Wolfgang van Emden, David Williams